Every Man

*Why Violence Against Women is a
Men's Issue, and How You Can
Make a Difference*

DR JACKSON KATZ

PENGUIN LIFE

AN IMPRINT OF

PENGUIN BOOKS

PENGUIN LIFE

UK | USA | Canada | Ireland | Australia
India | New Zealand | South Africa

Penguin Life is part of the Penguin Random House group of companies
whose addresses can be found at global.penguinrandomhouse.com

Penguin Random House UK,
One Embassy Gardens, 8 Viaduct Gardens, London SW11 7BW

penguin.co.uk
global.penguinrandomhouse.com

Penguin
Random House
UK

First published 2025

001

Set in 12.5/14.75pt Garamond MT Std
Typeset by Jouve (UK), Milton Keynes
Printed and bound in Great Britain by Clays Ltd, Elcograf S.p.A.

The authorized representative in the EEA is Penguin Random House Ireland,
Morrison Chambers, 32 Nassau Street, Dublin D02 YH68

A CIP catalogue record for this book is available from the British Library

ISBN: 978–0–241–67266–2

Penguin Random House is committed to a sustainable future
for our business, our readers and our planet. This book is made from
Forest Stewardship Council® certified paper.

MIX
Paper | Supporting
responsible forestry
FSC® C018179

Every Man

'Unflinchingly honest, *Every Man* equips men with the tools to become true allies. Katz doesn't offer empty promises or performative gestures; instead, he lays out the concrete actions every man can take to help dismantle gender violence. This is the handbook our culture so desperately needs' Jameela Jamil

'Bold but deeply rooted in compassion, Katz's writing offers us a road map too compelling to ignore. This is the kind of wisdom you feel inspired to study over and over again' Gina Martin

'We need more men to speak up and to speak out against gender-based violence or else, to state the glaringly obvious, nothing is going to change. Now more than ever, Katz's voice on this issue is vital. He is precise and intentional with his language while highlighting so powerfully the role that men must play in addressing the epidemic of male violence that we are currently facing. True allyship can be hard to come by in this area and harder still to define, but Katz has laid out a blueprint for what men can do and is leading by example. An important book at a critical time' Emma-Louise Boynton

'A must-read for men who want to learn more about what they can do to end violence against women' Professor Nicole Westmarland, Durham University Centre for Research into Violence and Abuse

'The violence that some men commit against women and girls is an issue for *all* men: it harms the women and girls we love, gives all men a bad name and hurts our communities. Jackson Katz invites every man to have the courage to speak up and challenge this abuse. Katz is an outstanding educator and thought leader, and this book provides essential tools, language and action for making change' Professor Michael Flood, author of *Engaging Men and Boys in Violence Prevention*

'In this timely and urgent book, Jackson Katz calls on men to confront the uncomfortable truths about male violence. He offers a practical and transformative blueprint for those who want to play a crucial role in promoting safe, healthy relationships. Katz's efforts have sparked a movement not only in North America but globally. I urge all men – especially those who love the women in their lives – to read this book and reflect on the critical role they can play in breaking the cycle of violence' Deeyah Khan, BAFTA and Emmy Award-winning film-maker and human rights activist

'This book is a powerful starter guide for men who are willing to challenge the roots of misogyny within themselves and society. Katz calls on men to take accountability and be active allies in ending violence against women and girls, which we have all been asking for. The book I'm going to give to the men in my life who are at the beginning of their journey into understanding feminism' Patsy Stevenson

ABOUT THE AUTHOR

Dr Jackson Katz is an American educator, speaker and writer who is internationally renowned for his groundbreaking work on issues of gender, race and violence. His TEDx Talk 'Violence Against Women – It's a Men's Issue' has been watched over 5.5 million times. He co-founded the pioneering gender violence prevention programme Mentors in Violence Prevention (MVP), which was the first large-scale prevention initiative in sports culture and all branches of the US military, and has been rolled out in schools across the US and parts of the UK. *Every Man* is his first book for a general reader.

For survivors, healers, advocates and activists

Contents

Author's Note

I wrote this book about men's violence against women, and not the many other forms of gender-based violence. I refer throughout to some of those other types of abuse, such as anti-LGBTQ violence, or women's violence against men. They are all related to my subject, sometimes closely. But they are not my focus here. For the sake of brevity and practicality, I generally use the terms 'gender violence', 'gender-based violence' and 'GBV' in place of the clunkier 'men's violence against women'. I try to use gender-inclusive language whenever possible. That doesn't mean I use gender-neutral language, however. Men's violence against women is not a gender-neutral problem, so it doesn't make sense to talk about it in gender-neutral terms. One of the book's main themes is that all men have a role to play if we have any hope of significantly reducing the incidence of gender-based violence. This requires radical honesty and accountable language when we think, talk and write about masculinities, misogyny and violence – even if that language can sometimes be discomfiting or provoke a defensive reaction, along the lines of #NotAllMen. Also, many of my writing choices were dictated by the book's length. Gender-based violence is an expansive topic with far-reaching effects at all levels of society, culture and politics.

By contrast, from the beginning of this project the idea was to produce a short, concise, energetic book that could nonetheless challenge conventional wisdom and catalyse positive change.

Introduction

In 2021, Sarah Everard was abducted and murdered in London by a serving Metropolitan Police officer. This tragic event touched a cultural nerve, because the circumstances of her killing were not only horrific but also archetypal. A single woman, walking alone early in the evening, killed by a violent stranger. She took many of the precautions that women are taught. She wore bright clothing, took a well-lit route and was talking with her boyfriend on the phone. Her murder confirmed what so many women already knew: it's hard to feel safe *anywhere*. Many people of colour understandably were upset that it took the murder of a white woman to attract the bright glare of the media spotlight. Where was the uproar when women of colour went missing, or when their bodies were found after they'd been murdered by a man? Still, women of all races and ethnicities took to the streets and social media to say 'I can't stop thinking about Sarah Everard', because they could all relate to her so directly. The feeling was widespread that 'it could have been me'.

Soon after, my email and social media accounts began to light up with inquiries from journalists and podcasters in the UK. They wanted answers to two basic questions: Why is men's violence against women such a persistent problem everywhere? And what can men do about it? They were asking me because these questions have been at the centre of my work as an activist, educator and scholar since I was a university student in the early 1980s. As subsequent protest rallies made abundantly clear, multitudes of women – especially young women – had reached a point of deep frustration and anger about the ineffective response of cultural and political leadership to the age-old problem of misogynous violence. And there was a growing call for actionable solutions.

Around the same time that I was doing those media interviews, an exercise I had designed many years earlier, 'Sexual Assault in the Daily Routine', went viral for the third or fourth time on social media, receiving millions of views. The exercise involves drawing a line down the middle of a whiteboard and asking all the men in the room to list the things they do on a daily basis to avoid being sexually assaulted (usually nothing) on one side. Then, asking women the same question, and watching a long list cover up the entire other side of the board. Many women reported feeling seen and heard by this exercise, but it's worth noting that it was originally designed as a consciousness-raising experience *for men*. It was meant to help them see how terribly unfair it is that women's daily lives continue to be shaped by realistic fears of men's violence – and to catalyse a conversation about what men can do about it. The story of how this workshop-exercise-turned-viral-sensation was conceived is as good a place as any for me to share some personal background about what drove my passion and commitment toward these matters, and what I am setting out to do in this book.

Scroll back to the early 1980s, when I was a student journalist working for my large public university's daily newspaper. I had been writing a weekly opinion column from the beginning of my second year, but on occasion I was asked to cover news events. One sunny spring day in New England I was assigned to write a story about a demonstration for better lighting on campus that had been organized by a group of women students. They were calling for this basic public safety intervention in response to a reported rape that had happened at night, in a car park, on the outskirts of campus. In the vast majority of sexual assaults and rapes that take place on campus, the perpetrator is known to the victim. But this incident, occurring on the campus boundaries, was of the 'stranger danger' variety. And like so many events before and since, the media reports generated fear in the psyches of thousands of women, and an even greater degree than usual of hypervigilance about their personal safety.

For reasons I did not understand at the time, as I walked, notebook in hand, toward a loud group of sign-wielding women picketing in front of the student centre, I felt exhilarated and inspired by this public display of righteous anger and self-assertion. It was a real-life illustration of leadership in action – these women were standing up for themselves and fighting back. Everyone should have the right to walk across campus without the fear of being assaulted. Women, men, everyone! Years later, when I had the opportunity to look back at this moment, I was struck by the fact that I didn't recall feeling defensive, or personally attacked, as so many men today feel when women assert their basic rights and dignity. I might not have been self-aware enough at the time to know why, but I found it viscerally moving to see this group of women students protesting rape and misogyny.

Why did this have such an impact on me? On the surface, I had conventional credentials in 'guyland'. I was white, heterosexual, a former star American football player in high school. I was enjoying my freedom to come and go at all hours of the day and night. I might have been a bit reckless, but like most white men in my cohort, I barely gave a moment's thought to my personal safety as I staggered back to my dorm after raucous keg parties, at three or four o'clock in the morning. It was great to be a white, middle-class university student more than a hundred miles from home! But even in this position of privilege, I could see that something wasn't right. I lived in a co-ed residence hall, and I started to notice that the women next door and across the hall were having a very different experience of 'freedom'. When they were out and about, especially at night, they had to worry constantly about what time it was, where they were, how they were getting home, and with whom. I remember thinking that if I were a woman and had to live like that, I'd be pretty furious about it too – and that's an understatement. I was vaguely aware of the Reclaim the Night rallies that had started in the UK in the late 1970s, where feminists organized night-time marches through the streets of Leeds and other cities to protest against men's violence toward women – protests that then spread to the US. But seeing this picket line on my own campus prompted me to start thinking seriously – for the first time in my life – about women's vulnerability to men's violence and their visceral fear of men, whether at home or on the streets. I wrote these thoughts up into a short piece for the paper called 'A Man Can Only Imagine'.

Fast-forward ten years. As an emerging leader in the growing multiracial, multiethnic movement of men working to end men's violence against women, I had just begun to receive speaking invitations from universities and high schools across North America—specifically to address both the ways in which entertainment media and other forces in male culture contributed to misogyny, and how men could be part of the solution. As I write this today, I have delivered thousands of talks in front of almost every imaginable audience inside and outside of academia. I've lectured at hundreds of prestigious universities in North America, and many more in Europe, South Africa, India, Hong Kong, Australia and elsewhere. I've trained non-commissioned officers as well as junior and senior military leaders on three continents about men's leadership in gender violence prevention, and shared my thoughts on the subject with thousands of cadets at all the US military academies. I've addressed numerous gatherings of both junior and senior business executives and leaders of organized labour. I've provided testimony in the United States Congress and participated in a UK parliamentary inquiry on commercial sexual exploitation. I've conducted trainings with male indigenous leaders in the US, Canada and Australia. I've presented my views at black-tie fundraisers in posh hotel ballrooms, and from makeshift podiums set up on sticky dance floors in military beer halls.

But when I was just starting out, I had to decide how I could be most effective in front of an audience. I wanted to reach men (and everyone else) with something more than clever rhetorical points or poignant insights. I wanted them to react viscerally, as I had when I began to learn more about this disturbing subject. This was still many years before digital technology and social media would make possible the world-changing revelations of #MeToo, or powerful initiatives like the Everyday Sexism Project, which Laura Bates created as an online forum for women (and others) to report the wide range of misogynous violations they have endured from men in their personal and professional lives. But long before the Digital Era, it was already obvious that making the issues personal was a powerful way to reach people.

I knew how powerful it had been for me to hear women's personal stories. Some of these were tearful testimonies from survivors at public events. At conferences and Reclaim the Night rallies from my university days onward, I listened to numerous women across the lifespan tell sad and sometimes shocking stories about their experiences of incest, rape and domestic abuse. I also heard many disturbing stories in private conversations.

As I grew more immersed in this work, especially after I graduated from university, I started to notice the multitude of media headlines about men assaulting women. A young mother stabbed to death by an ex-boyfriend as her kids wailed in the next room. A university student gang-raped by a group of men at an off-campus house party. A popular male athlete charged with sexual assault. If you paid even minimal attention to the news, you'd see these tragedies happening all the time. If you gave the subject the slightest bit of reflection, you'd notice that these cases were not 'isolated' events, but rather part of a much larger pattern. Because I travelled a lot, I also heard innumerable local stories that never made the national news. At one of my earliest high-school speaking events, when I was thirty, a sixteen-year-old girl in the front row had a black eye from a punch in the face by her boyfriend. (The organizers warned me about this beforehand, but I still had a tough time not staring.) Throughout all of this, I felt increasingly responsible *as a man* to speak out about this ongoing crisis, and to convey a sense of urgency to the growing numbers of people who attended my talks – especially the young men.

I began to search for a way to illustrate the depth and scope of the problem without using impersonal statistics. However dramatic and revelatory they might be, stats couldn't bring to life the personal toll that living with violence takes on women. I settled on a strategy that social justice educators had practised in the classroom for years: Bring large social issues to life by making them personal. Make the abstract concrete. Use examples.

Building on earlier feminist consciousness-raising efforts, the exercise I came up with began by drawing a line down the middle of a chalkboard or whiteboard. I would ask the men in the room a simple question: 'What steps do you take on a daily basis to avoid being sexually assaulted?' There often was audible laughter at the question, but mostly no one raised their hand. Sometimes a young guy would crack a joke about 'staying outta prison'. Eventually someone would say what most were thinking: 'I don't do anything. I don't even think about it.' I would leave the men's side blank. Then I would ask the women exactly the same question, only this time dozens of hands would shoot up. As the men sat in stunned silence, the women would call out a seemingly endless checklist of the things they did in their daily routine: hold your keys as a potential weapon; never put your drink down at a club or party; make sure the doors are locked when you're inside the car or house; never take a ground-floor apartment; look men in the eye as you pass them on the street; don't look men in the eye as you pass them on the street; use your first initial on the post box; don't wear headphones when jogging outside; and on and on. The women's side of the board would fill up as quickly as I could write the items down. And this list didn't even include all the things women might do in public spaces not only to reduce their risk of sexual assault, but also to avoid what the Durham University researcher Fiona Vera-Gray calls 'intrusions' by men into women's everyday lives – on the streets, aboard subway trains, in parks and a multitude of other places.

The stark contrast between the empty men's side and the jam-packed women's side made a powerful visual statement about the persistence of gender inequality. Many women who wanted to believe we lived in a 'post-feminist' era were upset by this contrary evidence; clearly not all the battles had 'already been won'. But the main point of the exercise was to show men, straight from the mouths of the women seated next to them, how unfair and unjust it was that women had to order their daily lives and schedules around the realistic fear of men's violence. In the lively discussions afterwards, I asked the men how they would feel if they had to take these sorts of steps every single day. I also made sure to acknowledge that men are sexually assaulted as well, and that some men do take daily precautions – despite the empty men's side of the board. But most don't. And the ones that do usually take steps to avoid being assaulted by other men.

'Sexual Assault in the Daily Routine' is one of several remedial empathy exercises I designed to help men relate at a gut level to women's experience of sexism. Since the early 1990s, my colleagues and I have used these exercises thousands of times in talks and trainings. The point is to humanize and personalize the topic, which in turn can help reduce men's reflexive defensiveness, especially when they encounter women's anger at having to live in a culture where violent misogyny is so pervasive. This sort of awareness-raising also serves a practical purpose. If a key goal of prevention work is to help men find the self-confidence and courage to speak out and challenge misogynous abuse by their fellow men, in the face of the inevitable pushback they get from their peers when they do so, we have to appeal to their hearts, not just their heads. I was confident this approach would work for others, because that's how it had worked for me.

When I was in graduate school in 1992, I approached Dr Richard Lapchick with an idea. Lapchick was the director of the Center for the Study of Sport in Society, an institute at Northeastern University in Boston, Massachusetts. He was also a prominent international figure in sport and civil rights activism, and created the centre in 1984 to further the goal of using sport as a vehicle for social justice activism.

I proposed to him my idea of creating a programme to train university male student athletes to speak out about men's violence against women.

The reason I was drawn to sports culture to do this work was simple – and it wasn't because male athletes are more likely to assault women. I was convinced – then as now – that millions of men love and care about women and are genuinely appalled by the harassment and violence women experience from men. The hard part is getting them to *do* something about it. One of the dirty little secrets of male culture is that men – young and old – worry so much about what other men think of them that they often tacitly accept – or even participate in – behaviour that makes them uncomfortable, including misogynous behaviour, rather than risk social disapproval. I was long aware of this dynamic, so I reasoned that one solution was for men who already had status to break the ice. If men – especially young men – saw that men they looked up to and admired were willing to stand with women and take on this issue, it would become easier for them to do so as well.

That's where sport came in. Sport is a pervasively influential institution that cuts across all the social categories of ethnicity, race, education, socioeconomics and geography. It is hardly a secret that successful male athletes tend to have enhanced status in the community, and thus have a bigger platform and a louder mouthpiece from which to exercise cultural influence. There was and remains a serious problem of sexist abuse at all levels of sport, from the junior level to the professional ranks, and it includes players and coaches, administrators and owners.

But I was more interested in sport as part of the *solution* rather than part of the *problem*.

With initial funding from the US government, we created the Mentors in Violence Prevention (MVP) programme, which today remains one of the longest-running and most widely influential programmes in the gender violence prevention field. By design, the model moved beyond sport into broader university and high school populations after the first few years. It also grew from an exclusive focus on men to become mixed-gender. In 1997, I started an iteration of MVP within the United States Marine Corps, the first system-wide gender violence prevention initiative in the United States Department of Defense. Eventually we expanded to all the uniformed services in the US military. MVP was also the first programme in North America to train professional athletes and the front-office staff of professional teams. The first such training we conducted was with the future dynastic champion New England Patriots American football club in 1999. To this day, MVP trainings – and those done by a number of spin-off programmes – are conducted regularly in schools, universities and workplaces large and small, in North America, the UK, Europe and Australia. To cite one relevant example, nearly every school district in Scotland runs MVP as their main school violence-prevention programme.

One of MVP's signature accomplishments is the introduction of the 'bystander' approach to the gender violence prevention field in the early 1990s. This now broadly popular educational strategy – which features throughout this book – combines the conceptual and practical dimensions of change. I describe this in much greater detail in chapter 6, but the animating idea behind bystander training is that everyone in a given peer culture – friends, classmates, teammates, colleagues, co-workers – has a role to play before, during and after instances of sexual harassment, assault or domestic abuse. This focus on the bystander represented a historic shift in gender violence prevention theory and practice. In the early days of the anti-rape movement in the 1970s and 1980s, most prevention education relied on the classic victim–perpetrator binary. The intent was to teach and empower potential victims (usually women) to protect and/or stand up for themselves, especially by avoiding or minimizing risk, or leaving abusive relationships. On the flip side, potential abusers (usually men) were encouraged to know the laws regarding sexual consent and domestic battery, and to back off if they were about to enter any sort of grey zone – sexually or otherwise – in which it wasn't clear whether it was okay to continue.

The new focus on the bystander upended the old binary. Now the spotlight was on what everyone else could do to 1) provide support to victims/survivors, 2) interrupt or challenge abusers and 3) help create and sustain a climate in the group that discouraged people from causing harm to others. And not because that behaviour was illegal or would result in repercussions from external agents of authority, but because it was unacceptable to members of the group itself.

The extensive work that I and my MVP colleagues have done over the years with young men, women and others across the ethnic/racial and socioeconomic spectrum has provided me with an enormous database of anecdotes and insights about what works and what doesn't, in terms of motivating people – especially men – to play an active role in changing the social norms that fuel misogyny. Much of what I share in this book comes directly from what I and my colleagues have learned in MVP trainings over the years, right through to the present.

Women's activism and leadership on the issue of gender-based violence have chipped away at the deeply entrenched misogyny in this society and around the world over the past few decades. Since long before #MeToo, a multiethnic, multiracial movement led by women has pushed govern-ments to fund programmes for victims and survivors, to reform and improve laws regarding offender accountability, and has challenged the cultural practices and social norms that help to perpetuate sexist harassment, abuse and to violence. They've made remarkable progress – even if there is still a long way to go. But we are approaching an inflection point on these matters, because a younger generation of women – from Manchester to Melbourne, Tehran to Texas – has made it clear that the status quo is unacceptable and unsustainable, and the appalling level of gender-based violence in the past and present is incompatible with minimal standards of a healthy and just society.

But what about men? Where have they been? Why don't more of them speak out? It's been years since #MeToo catapulted the issue of gender violence into the public consciousness. It's not as if men are unaware of the prob-lem. Untold millions of women and girls across the world have been harassed, abused or assaulted by men. The vast majority of these women and girls have men in their lives who love and care about them. Many of these men claim to hate violence and to support human rights and gender equality. So why has men's collective response to misogynous abuse and violence been so muted? Why is it still unusual to hear men in public life speak passionately about the urgent need to cut the high levels of men's violence against women? What's stopping them from doing so?

There are local and national organizations of men who do good work on this issue, as well as international networks like the MenEngage Alliance; I'll discuss some of their efforts in these pages. In Australia, a spike in domestic homicides in 2024, and a man's killing spree in a Sydney mall in which five of his six victims were women, sparked a renewed national dialogue about the crisis of men's violence against women. Notably, the conversation included a special emphasis on the need for men – including men in positions of cultural influence and institutional and political power – to speak out *and* back up their words with long-term plans for concrete action and the funding to make it possible. Nonetheless, there has never been even a fledgling mass movement of men – in the US, the UK, Australia, or anywhere else in the world – dedicated to stamping out this continuing scourge. I have written this book in part as an attempt to figure out why, and to offer solutions and a viable path forward. In the chapters that follow, I will analyse and reframe the problem, and then go on to outline concrete strategies for action.

In chapter 1, I will ask you to join me in thinking about this ancient issue in a new, contemporary way. Chapter 2 looks at the ways in which blaming victims and describing men who use violence in their relationships as monsters are two sides of the same coin: they both serve to deflect our attention away from the fact that most gender violence is committed by otherwise normal men. Chapter 3 looks at the normalization of gender violence in our societies by examining two critical sources of influence in the sexual psyches of young men: porn culture, and the misogynous manfluencer Andrew Tate. Chapter 4 will share the most common (and predictable) objections people raise to the arguments I put forth in the book. I will show you how to dismantle those arguments. In chapter 5, I focus on the power of language; I call for an overhaul of the ways in which we think, speak and write about this topic. Chapter 6 introduces you to the bystander approach to sexual assault and relationship abuse prevention. As one of the early architects of this strategy, which is now growing in popularity in the UK, Australia and parts of Europe, I'll give you some background and specific scenarios to walk you through the philosophy and methods of my teaching on this dynamic approach to prevention. I will show you how you can step in and make a difference, strongly and safely. Chapter 7 argues that gender violence prevention is ultimately a responsibility for leaders – with a special focus on male leaders. Leadership can be formal or informal. If you're a man who's a leader among your peers, or if you occupy a position of educational, political, cultural or business leadership, you'll find some guidance about how to exercise that leadership effectively. The final chapter features a list of concrete steps for individuals, organizations, businesses and governments, followed by a redefinition of men's strength, along with an urgent call to action.

Over the past forty years, one of the primary mantras

in the gender violence prevention field has been the need to 'raise awareness'. But I'm not interested in awareness-raising for its own sake. It might be a necessary first step, but we've been there and done that. I'm an educator, but here's a spoiler alert: the overarching answer I put forth in these pages isn't simply to provide more education. No matter how important it is to know the warning signs of abuse in relationships, refute rape myths and educate everyone about consent – especially men – much more is needed. The goal now needs to be much more ambitious. It needs to focus on action – personal, institutional and political – to change the social norms that underlie misogynous abuse.

One of the biggest stumbling blocks to that over the last few decades has been the reticence of 'good guys' to embrace this issue as theirs to solve. Of course, it's necessary to critique and counter openly sexist men – whether it's garden-variety right-wing anti-feminists, or more notorious misogynists like Gamergate bros, incels, and online manfluencers like Andrew Tate – and there will be plenty of that in this book. But in some ways, calling out 'toxic masculinity' is too easy; it's the low-hanging fruit. I am even more interested in seeking explanations for why millions of otherwise supportive, conscious, twenty-first-century men have been so slow to mobilize around these issues. In this book, I will provide these men with the tools to think about this issue in a new way, but also propose strategies for putting these ideas into practice. We clearly still have a lot of work ahead of us. The good news is that not only do we know a lot about why this continues to be such a problem, we also know a great deal about the personal and political barriers to transformative change. And we have some very good ideas about solutions, both for institutions and for individuals, whatever the size and scope of their sphere of influence. You will find all of that in these pages, along with a challenge to men especially: we can and must do better.

1. W̶o̶Men's Issues

'There is a real consensus that men must
play their part if we are to achieve true
parity between the sexes.'
– Julia Gillard, former prime minister of Australia

The United States government defines gender-based violence as 'any harmful threat or act directed at an individual or group based on actual or perceived sex, gender, gender identity or expression, sex characteristics, sexual orientation, and/or lack of adherence to varying socially constructed norms around masculinity and femininity'. Although individuals of all gender identities may experience gender-based violence, 'women, girls, and gender non-conforming individuals face a disproportionate risk of gender-based violence across every context due to their unequal status in society'.

Notably, this definition does not say that men are responsible for the vast majority of the violence. It says that *women, girls, and gender non-conforming individuals* face a disproportionate risk of gender-based violence, but it doesn't say that *men, young men, and boys* face a disproportionate risk of committing it. This crucial point is frequently glossed over when people use the passive phrase 'violence against women', as if it's a bad thing that simply *happens* to women. No one is *doing* it to them; they're just experiencing it, kind of like the weather. When you insert the word 'men' you have a new phrase: 'men's violence against women'. It doesn't roll off the tongue as easily, but it's more accurate and honest. How are we supposed to solve this enormous and vexing problem if we're not even willing to say out loud who's responsible for it?

In addition, discussions about this topic rarely include analyses about its systemic nature. Gender violence perpetration is more commonly described as the province of disturbed individuals – the sick or depraved men who do awful things to women they claim to love, or random women they meet online or on the street. To be sure, disturbed individuals are responsible for a portion of the problem. But the sheer volume of this violence means it can't be understood as the deviant behaviour of individuals. The mass rape case in southern France that stunned the world in 2024 illustrated this in dramatic fashion. A man previously described as a loving husband and father, Dominique Pelicot, was charged with drugging his wife of fifty years, Gisele, and arranging for a succession of men to rape her while she was unconscious. Authorities charged fifty men with raping her over a ten-year period. They ranged in age from twenty-six to sixty-eight, many of them married with children. The ordinary nature of the alleged perpetrators – business owners, forklift drivers, firefighters, soldiers, journalists – made it impossible to dismiss them as pathological outliers.

The unpleasant reality is that gender violence across a wide spectrum – from catcalls on the street to femicide – is a perpetual occurrence in virtually every community – rich and poor; urban, suburban and rural. It's devastatingly common throughout the developing world and in all the wealthy countries as well, including the UK and the rest of Europe. Even Scandinavia! In fact, misogynous violence is one of the oldest problems in our species, and unfortunately a feature, not a bug, of patriarchal societies.

The rates of men's violence against women – sexual harassment, rape, domestic abuse, commercial sexual exploitation and a host of other gender-related crimes – continue to shock the conscience. According to Rape Crisis England and Wales, more than 6.5 million women over the age of sixteen have been raped or sexually assaulted. On average, a woman is murdered by her husband, boyfriend or ex once every three days. In the US, domestic abuse hotlines receive 19,000 calls on a typical day, and one in four women experiences physical violence, sexual violence and/or stalking from an intimate partner in her lifetime. During the COVID-19 pandemic, evidence suggests that there were spikes in the incidence and severity of domestic abuse, and dramatic increases in the number of calls to helplines. A recent survey found that 80 per cent of women in the UK had been sexually harassed in public spaces, a number that increased to 97 per cent for women aged 18–24. Women with disabilities are 2–4 times more likely than women without them to experience domestic abuse or sexual assault. One multinational study in 2020 found that more than one-third of respondents in the UK, Australia and New Zealand had experienced at least one form of image-based sexual abuse victimization, such as the non-consensual sharing of nudes or sexual images; women in their twenties were the most common victims. These alarming statistics are hardly attributable to abusive or antisocial behaviour by a small number of 'toxic' men. At this point, it is silly for any honest person to pretend this is anything other than a deeply rooted societal problem.

I called my viral TEDx Talk 'Violence Against Women – It's a Men's Issue' for a reason. Even if people don't want to take the seventeen minutes to watch it, the title itself makes the central point. There is simply no way to solve the problem of violence against women unless we figure out better ways to engage and mobilize men. How do we do that? First, we have to challenge old and stale habits of thought that have long held us back. One of the biggest is the misguided notion that because only *some* men commit overt acts of violence against women, it's not really something *all* men need to think about. Isn't that why it's called a *women's issue*?

Gender violence is a societal scourge that has persisted for thousands of years, despite the countless women (and some men) who have fought long and hard against it both as individuals and within women-led movements, and whose efforts have accelerated dramatically over the past half-century. These efforts have resulted in measurable progress, most notably in terms of enhanced public consciousness about the extent of the problem, improvements in the provision of services to victims and survivors, and increased accountability for those who cause harm and injury. Nonetheless, the problem persists.

In the starkest of terms, too many people tend to regard gender-based violence as something unfortunate that *happens* to women, rather than something men *do* to them. It seems to me that flipping the script of that specific narrative is essential if we are going to make major progress in the struggle to end this violence. In other words, any real hope of achieving dramatic reductions in the enormously high global rates of men's violence against women requires a radical revision of the very way in which we understand this vexing topic. Despite more awareness of the issue in recent years, this remains the same today. In fact, if you remember nothing else from this book, I want this to be your main takeaway: instead of thinking of gender violence as a women's issue that more 'good men' should help out with, we need to understand it as a men's issue. As a matter of universal human rights that every man of integrity and sense of personal and/or political responsibility has no choice but to grapple with – and do something about. And not just when women raise the issue.

In his classic book *The Gender Knot*, the sociologist Allan Johnson explains that men can support individual women without doing anything to challenge or undermine their own privilege or raise these issues with other men. These men can be drawn into defining problems such as housework, workplace discrimination, sexual harassment and gender violence as 'women's issues', which makes it easy for them to see themselves as loving helpers, loyal supporters or valiant defenders of women. Yet men, Johnson writes, rarely take the initiative on these crucial matters. Instead, they leave it to women to decide what needs to be 'said, asked, listened to, discussed, fought over, attended to, and cared for' in overcoming the 'status quo's foot-dragging inertia'.

In other words, part of what has been missing is anti-sexist leadership from men on both personal and political levels. If more men would take this sort of initiative and provide leadership, it would not only help to create a more equitable and safer world, but also ease some of the pressure on women and reduce the risk they often face when they speak out and demand action in the face of misogyny and injustice. This requires a fundamental shift in consciousness, but it's a shift whose seeds were planted by visionary activists and writers nearly half a century ago.

The Will to Change

The late Black feminist cultural critic bell hooks wrote that just as white people have a crucial role to play in the struggle against racism, men have a primary role to play in eradicating sexism. hooks argued this is their duty as a matter of basic human rights and dignity, much in the same way that it is for whites who believe in fundamental principles of fairness and justice. But she also famously — and counterintuitively — maintained that working toward gender equality is in men's self-interest, because the patriarchal system that causes unspeakable harm to women also does tremendous damage to boys and men. Working for women's rights will improve men's lives as well. The possibilities for dramatic social transformation would increase measurably if men were to develop what she called a 'will to change', in part because it would nearly double the number of people with a direct stake in that change.

Notably, hooks was an African American woman who, like so many women of colour in the movements against gender violence, was not willing to dismiss men as a monolithic and irredeemable oppressor class — precisely because those women were standing side by side with men in their communities in the fight against racism. To this day, some of the most enthusiastic support for working with male allies in the struggle against gender violence comes from women of colour, immigrant women and others from marginalized communities.

Whose Issue is This?

Efforts to engage and mobilize men begin with acknowledging that the very act of calling violence against women a 'women's issue' is itself part of the problem. Why? Because it takes the focus off the group committing the violence and puts it onto the one experiencing it. Shifting accountability from the group with more power onto the group with less is one of the many subtle ways in which dominant groups insulate themselves from criticism or challenges to their power. As long as the spotlight remains on the people to whom bad things are happening, less attention is paid to those who are doing it to them. The same process applies to a range of issues related to social and economic inequality. To describe violence against women as a 'women's issue' is like saying that racism is an issue for people of colour, or that homophobia is an issue for LGBTQ people. The linguistic sleight of hand does its work by absolving those with the power to marginalize and oppress. In societies that have been male-dominated for millennia, one of the most important questions we should be asking is: what can men do to end violence against women? But how can we answer that question when we continue to focus on the violence women experience without even mentioning who's doing it to them?

Calling gender violence a 'women's issue' also doesn't

account for the many ways in which men are harmed by other men's violence against the women they love. Everything that happens to women in a sense also happens to men, because we live in the world together. Our lives are inextricably interwoven. Obviously, there are some ways in which a person's biological sex or gender identity will make certain issues more salient for them. But in the case of gender violence, even though women are its primary victims and men the vast majority of perpetrators, men and boys are impacted negatively in countless ways. One of the clearest examples of this is the boys who are traumatized by what an adult man – their father or another man – does to their mother.

We have decades of research and personal testimony from boys who have experienced this abuse directly in their families, many of whom are now grown men. Some of them are famous, like the British actor Patrick Stewart and the South African comedian Trevor Noah, both of whom watched and experienced men in their families assaulting their mothers, and both of whom have used their public platform to speak out about domestic abuse and rally men to the cause. The brothers Luke and Ryan Hart from Lincolnshire have made it their life's work to campaign to end domestic violence, in honour of their mother Claire and nineteen-year-old sister Charlotte, who were murdered by their father. These exceptional men and so many others carry their experiences of trauma and loss into adulthood, often at serious cost to their emotional, psychological and physical health – and their ability to develop and sustain healthy relationships. Stewart said that he hadn't really faced his childhood trauma until he was in therapy, during the *Star*

Trek years, when he lived in California. 'I was ashamed and embarrassed — and that embarrassment went all the way back to being seven or eight. At the time, our tightly knit community knew what my father did to my mother — they could hear it — but it was absolutely not talked about. Even with my brothers, we didn't discuss it. I think we tried to pretend it wasn't there.'

Countless men throughout the world love and care deeply about women and girls in their lives who have been sexually abused, assaulted and harassed by men. I meet these men all the time after my talks, in the middle of trainings or through online communication. They're members of an informal brotherhood of men who are closely connected to survivors. I'm a member of the brotherhood — as are most of the men I know! If someone started a global support group devoted exclusively to the needs of fathers of female rape victims/survivors, its membership could grow into the hundreds of millions. No one can tell me that rape isn't an issue for those men. To be sure, women and girls are the primary victims and survivors of the harassment, abuse and violence that men do to them. But they're not the only ones.

We can debate about the best ways to proceed, but it's naive to think we can continue to label gender violence a 'women's issue' and hope that will suffice. In male-dominated societies, this is a classic way of devaluing the matter at hand. It's not a giant leap from 'it's a women's issue' to 'it's *only* a women's issue', because historically — and in many ways right up to the present — women's lives have been regarded as less important than men's. In Western democracies, women have been fighting for centuries merely to be considered full citizens with equal protection of the law. That is why then US First Lady Hillary Rodham Clinton's declaration that 'women's rights are human rights' at the 1995 World Conference on Women in Beijing was such a groundbreaking moment. Three decades later, this now-iconic quote might seem like a statement of the obvious. But it struck a deep chord with women all over the world precisely because it posed a direct challenge to thousands of years of conventional wisdom.

The courageous leadership of women has always been the driving force for change. This includes the inspired leadership of countless survivors, ranging from those who are known only in their small circles or local communities, all the way to the rich and famous. These women regularly demonstrate incredible bravery in their willingness to speak truth to power, and in many cases risk further injury by talking openly about what men have done to them – despite many people not believing them or wanting them to keep their experiences to themselves. Any serious effort to address gender violence needs to amplify the voices of survivors, as well as to design survivor-centred systems of advocacy and response. But it's simply unfair to expect survivors to be leading efforts to change the social norms that drive perpetration; they already have their hands full.

While women's leadership created and has sustained the movements against gender violence, the idea that women are primarily responsible for 'solving' this deeply rooted problem unduly burdens the group of people who are its worst victims, even as it evades the stark reality that the vast majority of sexual and domestic abuse is perpetrated by men – whether the victims of this violence are women, men or members of marginalized communities such as those who are LGBTQ. Quite simply, it seems fair to ask: are women assaulting themselves? If not, then why should they bear the primary responsibility for stopping men from doing harmful things to them, or remaking cultural belief systems about masculinity or male entitlement? Don't they have enough to do already?

According to feminist author Laura Bates, when it comes to redefining masculinity, the bulk of the work needs to be done by men. By expecting feminist women to tell boys the right way to be a man, she says, the 'hard work has been foisted on the wrong people'. Moreover, why should we expect men merely to be supportive *allies* to women, instead of shouldering the lion's share of the burden themselves? As if it's fundamentally a women's fight that we need to help them wage. Why shouldn't the onus of responsibility and leadership on this matter reside primarily with men, especially those men who – for reasons of socioeconomic status, race and class – have disproportionate economic, political and social power and influence?

Activists and professionals in the gender-based violence (GBV) field have wrestled with a number of ethical conundrums for the past couple of decades. For example, tensions are bound to arise if the primary goal in established programmes and NGOs is to empower women, and yet at the same time a growing number of people are calling for a dramatic expansion of efforts to engage men and boys. Does an increased emphasis on work with men require redirecting resources away from women? And how can men be leaders in the struggle against gender violence and not reinforce the idea – bluntly or subtly – that men are once again the actors driving change? This can be even more of a challenge for conscientious anti-sexist white men, who not only are relentlessly mocked as 'cucks' and 'betas' in the online manosphere, but also are wary of being derided as white male saviours by activists on their own side. I've wrestled with these sorts of dilemmas for years. Criticism from fellow activists can sometimes be frustrating, but it is surely fair to ask how men in general – and white men especially – can be leaders on this topic without engaging in patronizing and sexist chivalry, or encroaching on women's spaces and opportunities to lead.

There is also the question of whether it is productive to use gender-specific remedies or language at all. Why use traditional binary categories? When sexual and intimate partner abuse affects everyone across the gender identity spectrum, why is it necessary to say this is either a men's issue *or* a women's issue? Why not use gender-neutral terminology, such as calling it a public health, human rights or social justice issue? I heard this complaint almost from the moment I started writing and speaking about this topic. Wasn't the very act of gendering the discussion about sexual and domestic abuse inherently divisive – meaning it would alienate men? Wasn't it also inaccurate, because didn't I know that women can be abusive too? Sometimes this attempt to depoliticize the issue by degendering it came from people who were genuinely concerned that it would be harder to help people in need if it became another skirmish in the 'battle of the sexes'. Sometimes the impetus came from 'men's rights' activists, who have been trying to undermine the feminist-led movements against domestic and sexual violence for decades, through attempts to convince the general public of a highly misleading and false equivalence – that women abuse men as often as men abuse women. In recent years, the impetus for gender-neutral language more broadly has also come from the transgender movement, whose rationale is that using such language fosters inclusivity.

Whatever the motivation, the use of gender-neutral language to describe gender violence doesn't get us any closer to solving the problem – it moves us further away. Gender violence is not a gender-neutral problem. Men – not 'people' – commit the vast majority of sexual harassment, sexual assault, domestic abuse, child sexual abuse, commercial sexual exploitation, etc. – regardless of the sex or gender identity of the victims. It seems worth the effort to explore the reasons why. Of course, women can also be abusive and violent, as can non-binary people. But gender neutrality, in this particular matter, requires a wilful denial of reality – the underlying imbalance of power between the sexes in male-dominated societies, and the stark social and relational inequalities that result. If the true source of the problem were dysfunctional 'people' in relationships, there would be no need to critically examine – and change – traditional hierarchies or the institutional practices that maintain the status quo.

One can apply similar logic to the 'All Lives Matter' mantra recited by right-wing elements in response to Black Lives Matter. The idea behind BLM is that racism devalues Black life; hence the need for the corrective assertion that Black lives matter. Saying 'all lives matter' negates the specificity of anti-Black racism and violence and the urgent need to address it, which depoliticizes the issue and thus drains the movement of its animating energy. If 'all lives matter', the fight against racial injustice loses its urgency, especially with regard to extrajudicial and police-involved violence.

So it is with men's violence against women. If the problem is that individuals who engage in acts of abuse or violence are simply unhealthy, mentally unstable or otherwise maladjusted people, there is no need to question male dominance or any other underlying system. Just run from one incident of abuse to the next as if they're not connected – as if they're not predictable outcomes of unequal societal beliefs and practices around gender and power. Not coincidentally, framing the problem in this highly individualized and depoliticized way means that most men will continue to avert their eyes, and we'll be nowhere closer to solving the pervasive problems of misogyny and sexist violence.

Why Not All Men?

Although it might seem like a novel idea, the idea of framing gender violence prevention as 'men's work' has been around since at least the late 1970s, with the formation of a handful of small men's groups in the US, UK and elsewhere. Among the most notable was the multiracial Oakland Men's Project, which gave us the 'Act Like a Man Box', an exercise that is used to this day in violence prevention workshops around the world. In his 1992 book *Men's Work*, the project's co-founder Paul Kivel writes that in the early days of OMP, he and his colleagues began with a commitment to challenge violence against women, but soon realized this was more difficult to do than they initially thought. They needed to continually adapt their workshops to the needs of different populations and age groups, as well as confront their own prejudices and personal histories. 'As we understood more deeply what male violence is about, we moved toward a bigger challenge,' Kivel recalls. 'We not only aspired toward lives free from violence, we also wanted to create lives that were healthy, intimate with others, and models for our children. We aspired to help build stronger communities and to nurture the natural environment' – and create new and healthier ways of being men.

What Kivel, myself and others recognized many years ago is that ending men's violence against women means doing much more than simply telling men to stop doing it – or else. It means challenging deeply rooted belief systems that connect being a 'real man' with power and control – especially over women. This requires much more ambitious efforts than merely devising prevention programmes and other well-meaning initiatives run by small charities and non-governmental organizations with fragile sources of funding. It means transforming norms and practices in mainstream institutions like the media, schools, sports culture, religious institutions and the military. It means talking to and working with all men, not just the ones who have already been caught and punished for crimes against women. It means taking into account the many ethnic, racial, religious and socioeconomic differences between and among men – and not pretending that all men have the same life experiences, or that 'men' is a homogeneous category.

The idea is to push for more egalitarian and non-violent

definitions of manhood – at the cultural centre and not just the margins – and pass that down to younger men and boys. The ultimate goal is to help change cultural narratives about masculinity that equate strength in men with power over women and entitlement to their bodies. This was a highly ambitious undertaking in the 1970s, 1980s and early 1990s, especially once a cultural and political backlash formed in response to historic feminist challenges to male dominance in private and public life. Today, the social terrain in some ways appears even more daunting, with the backlash intensifying as a reaction to both women's gains and the increased recognition and societal acceptance of LGBTQ diversity. In the States, Donald Trump was elected president in 2016 despite a long record of misogynous statements and sexual assault allegations. In 2024, he was chosen by millions of voters to be the Republican nominee, and then elected president, even after he was found liable by a Manhattan jury in 2023 of sexually abusing and defaming a prominent writer; the judge in the case explained that what New York state law refers to as 'sexual abuse' is actually rape. In a tragic twist, the person he ended up defeating was Kamala Harris, whose career began as a criminal prosecutor handling child sexual abuse cases. And of course, while the internet and social media have provided women with an unprecedented platform and a voice to fight back against misogyny through world-changing initiatives like #MeToo, they have also made possible the anti-feminist backlash known as Gamergate in 2014, the creation and proliferation of the manosphere, and more recently the incredible and disturbing popularity of the charismatic and influential misogynist Andrew Tate.

Despite these obstacles – and the reality that we've got a long way to go – there is reason for cautious optimism. For one thing, the sheer volume of cultural conversations about the role of men in ending men's violence against women – as well as their intensity – has increased by orders of magnitude from when I was young in the 1970s and 1980s. It's also fair to say that those of us working to engage and mobilize men in order to reduce misogyny and all forms of men's violence against women have had some measurable successes. These include an outpouring of research and writing over the past generation that addresses men's lives and identities in all their multiracial, multiethnic complexity, as well as the ways in which certain ideas about 'manhood' are connected to different forms of violence, including gender-based violence; a marked increase in school- and university-based prevention programmes that focus on men, young men and boys; and a growing number of NGO, community, government and private-sector initiatives around the world that seek to end misogynous violence through the promotion of 'healthy masculinity' and the encouragement of social and emotional intelligence in boys and men. Still, all these years later, we have yet to convince a critical mass of men at every level of cultural and political leadership and influence that it is their responsibility *as men* to speak out and take action to end men's violence toward women. That it is less about being a nice guy than it is about being a strong, responsible man in the late twentieth and twenty-first centuries.

Alas, there are no quick fixes. Changing hearts, minds and social norms in meaningful ways can take decades and generations – as does changing the underlying economic and political structures that keep the status quo in place.

What makes the gender violence issue especially difficult is that millions of men – billions, really – love and care deeply about the women and girls in their lives, and often recoil at the implication that their actions or inactions might be causing them harm. It's much more comfortable to subscribe to the 'bad apples' theory of social problems, in which men's violence toward women is perpetrated by pathological individuals, rather than being a manifestation of gender inequality rooted in a deeper system of male dominance. You run into a classic roadblock when you start talking about systems in this way. Members of historically powerful or privileged groups have a tendency to resist introspection or even minimal self-criticism about the unjust ways in which they've maintained their advantage. 'I'm a good guy,' men will say. 'This isn't my problem!'

Allan Johnson said that this type of denial is intrinsic to unjust and unequal systems. The path of least resistance for members of any dominant group, he wrote, is to see themselves as not having to do anything. 'The status quo is organized in [men's] image and in their gender interests ... Why, then, change it? Why question, much less give up, what they've got and risk *men's* disapproval, anger, and rejection, not to mention feeling disempowered, diminished, and "softened" to a position of equality with women? And why should they do this when they may not feel terribly good about their own lives in the first place?'

Thankfully, some people in groups with more social power are ready to 'do the work' in spite of these sorts of disincentives. Think about the legions of white supporters who came out to Black Lives Matter rallies, the men who turned out in large numbers for global women's marches the day after Donald Trump became president of the United States in 2017, and the multitudes of straight allies of LGBTQ rights. But just as predictably, some people in dominant groups interpret calls for accountability as an attack on both their rights and their character. Witness the ongoing 'culture wars' in the States over schools teaching inconvenient truths about racism in American history. Much of the pushback comes from conservative white parents, who worry that their children will be made to feel guilty about the sins of slavery and the genocide of Native Americans by white European colonial settlers in centuries past. Similarly, one of the biggest hurdles in the effort to get men to see misogynous violence as their issue is that many people – including some women – regard this either as an illegitimate attempt to assign collective guilt or as outright man-bashing. In the face of this sort of resistance, it is not surprising that *men's* violence against women continues to be understood as a *women's* issue. It's much less threatening that way for many women, and especially for men.

And it was women, after all, who organized grassroots mobilizations to create domestic abuse shelters and rape crisis centres, starting in the 1970s. They identified and named the problem, located sources of funding, started programmes, pressed municipal and national governments to strengthen domestic abuse and sexual violence law – and instituted a host of other measures and reforms. The vast majority of – but by no means all – academic research on this topic has been done by women. The multiracial, multiethnic women-led movements against domestic abuse and sexual assault have utterly transformed the cultural landscape, sometimes in ways so profound that it's difficult to imagine how things used to be. Prior to the 1970s, the types of services and treatment for victims and survivors that are widely available today were virtually non-existent. Survivors didn't have any kind of collective public voice. Outside of high-profile incidents and scandals, violence against women was barely discussed, much less understood as a major social problem.

Similarly, over the years, governments at the local, regional and national levels – under sustained pressure from women's organizations – have instituted legal reforms that increase accountability for offenders. One of the most important is the criminalization of rape within marriage, which wasn't officially against the law in the UK until 1991! In the US, marital rape was only outlawed in all fifty states in 1993. A major reason why it took so long to change the law was the residual power of a common law doctrine developed by the seventeenth-century British jurist Matthew Hale, who infamously wrote that a 'husband cannot be guilty of a rape committed by himself upon his lawful wife, for by their mutual matrimonial consent and contract the wife hath given up herself in this kind to her husband which she cannot retract'.

Despite these regrettable cultural roots, over time the aforementioned reforms and other challenges to old patriarchal belief systems have contributed to a tectonic shift in popular consciousness about the acceptability of men's violence against women. Even before the #MeToo movement – founded initially by the American activist Tarana Burke in 2006 and reignited by the actress Alyssa Milano in 2017 – popular consciousness about the issue of gender violence had been undergoing a generational – and irreversible – transformation, due to courageous and tireless advocacy by women of every ethnic and racial background in the UK, in North America and all over the world.

It is possible to change people's perceptions – and their behaviour. Including men's. I know this from my own personal *and* professional experience. My colleagues and I in the Mentors in Violence Prevention programme – along with many other initiatives in the global 'engaging men' space – have facilitated robust dialogues with men and young men for decades. In MVP we often work in extremely traditional and hyper-masculine institutions like sport and the military. We have seen countless men go from a defensive posture to an activist anti-sexist stance – sometimes in a short period of time. Along the way, we've developed a number of effective strategies to engage and mobilize men. I have written this book in part to share some of those strategies, in an effort to help scale up and take this work to the next level. But even before we get to the nuts and bolts of what men can do, it's critical to set the right tone regarding the terms of their engagement.

Positive Steps to Change

From my earliest days as an activist educator, I knew that in order to make changes in social norms and institutional practices, we needed to get men invested, both as individuals and in their positions of influence within male-dominated institutions. Cultural transformation on the broad scale that's needed can never happen as long as men remain closed off in a defensive crouch, perpetually denying and deflecting responsibility. And it isn't just men's defensiveness that has to be overcome; sometimes it is women's.

I experienced the latter for the first time in the early 1990s, during the lead-up to a talk I was preparing to deliver at an all-school assembly at a public high school in a medium-sized town in New Hampshire. A woman active in the community had invited me to speak at the school – because, she told me, her daughter and some of her friends had been sexually harassed and bullied there by some of the boys. She said the place was hostile to girls and operated like an old boys' club, with little accountability for sexism by adults or kids. She had contacted me after hearing a story on Boston public radio about the programme I ran with university and high school athletes. She worked with the school administration and we got as far as scheduling a date. Then, a few weeks before the event, she called to tell me it had been cancelled. It turned out some mothers of sons in the school had learned that a man was coming to talk about violence against women, and they objected out of concern that I would be 'too hard on the boys'. That was the first of many times over the years – and it continues to happen today – in which my or my colleagues' work has been undermined or blocked by people who think efforts to engage men and boys in the struggle to address men's violence against women is somehow unfair – to men and boys.

I knew those boys' mothers were wrong about me and terribly short-sighted on the issue, but I used it as a wake-up call. Up to that point, I had figured that being a man with my background was enough to get me through the door – so to speak. But I realized that I and others needed to do more to work around that sort of defensive resistance. We could stress the urgency of the problem and simply point to the latest incident in the news as evidence of the harm men were doing to women and girls. But if we wanted cautious, conventional institutions like schools and sports culture to work with us, and ultimately become a force for change, we needed to articulate a more positive case for men's involvement. It's something I've done ever since. Here are four of the strategies I've used to set a tone that helps to accomplish this:

1. Directly address the difference between guilt and responsibility

Critics of efforts to achieve racial and gender justice often claim that white men who are active in those areas must be driven by some form of guilt: liberal guilt, white guilt, male guilt. It's as if they can't wrap their heads around the fact that some of us are motivated by a basic commitment to justice, fairness and non-violence. Or that there's a big difference between guilt and responsibility. Let me illustrate that difference by sharing what I tell audiences all over the world.

I don't feel guilty for being a man, or a white person, or for being heterosexual. That's silly. As far as I know, I was born that way. Why should I feel guilty about it? I'm neither proud nor ashamed of any of those features of my identity. But I do feel *responsible* for all of them. As a white person who believes in elementary principles of equality and democracy,

I feel that it's my responsibility to work for racial justice; if I wasn't doing that, I'd feel like a coward or a hypocrite. As someone who's heterosexual/heteronormative, I believe it's my responsibility to advocate for equal rights for LGBTQ people and against discrimination and violence toward them – especially since most of the violence comes from members of my group: men. And as a man in a society and world in which misogynous violence is pervasive, I feel it's my responsibility to do whatever I can to make the world a better, fairer and safer place for women and girls. Not because I'm perfectly non-sexist or have this all figured out. Far from it. Like everyone else, I'm a work in progress. But I feel that I should do whatever I can *because I'm a man* in a patriarchal society that gives me and other men unfair advantages that result in harm to others, not because I *personally* feel guilty. Moreover, feeling guilty doesn't accomplish much of anything. Guilt is not a motivating emotion. People who feel guilty are more likely to retreat and be ineffectual, whereas people animated by a sense of responsibility are more likely to do something constructive.

2. Introduce and explain the 'triad of men's violence'

Whenever women tell their stories about misogynous abuse, some men are quick to jump in with the familiar cry: 'What about violence against men?' This is classic whataboutism, but it also suggests a lack of understanding about the ways in which men's violence against women is deeply connected to men's violence against other men. They're interwoven and often mutually reinforcing. In fact, you can't really comprehend one if you don't know anything about the other.

People who do 'men's work' have long been explicit about the link. One of my first educational projects was an illustrated lecture about masculinities and violence that I developed in the early 1990s and presented on university campuses and at gender violence conferences. It was called 'My Gun's Bigger Than Yours: Images of Violence and Manhood in the Media'. It examined the ways in which cultural ideas and narratives about 'manhood' contribute to much of the violence men do – to others and themselves – and provided source material for my first educational documentary, *Tough Guise*.

The connection between men's violence against women and other types of violence was the subject of a brilliant 1987 essay by the Canadian-American author and activist Michael Kaufman, entitled 'The Construction of Masculinity and the Triad of Men's Violence'. Kaufman, who went on to co-found the groundbreaking, global men's gender violence prevention initiative the White Ribbon Campaign, identified three 'corners' of violence (the triad) that are mutually reinforcing: men's violence against women; men's violence against each other; and men's violence against themselves (suicide, which is violence turned inward). They're all deeply interconnected in both obvious and more subtle ways.

Put simply, the same system that produces men who abuse women produces men who use violence in other circumstances as well. The key similarity is that, in all cases, boys and men are trained to use violence as a means to an end, whether that is power, control, self-assertion, self-defense, self-harm or some other desired outcome. One reason why it's useful to point this out in the context of gender violence prevention work with men is that untold numbers of them have been victims of violence – often as children or adolescents – and usually at the hands of other boys and men. Practically speaking, this has the potential to increase their empathy with women's experience of men's violence, because they can begin to see commonalities between their experience and what women go through.

3. Invite not indict men and boys

Many men feel defensive about this topic . . . and with good reason. Depending on how wide one casts the net in terms of how to define misogynous abuse, millions of men have taken part in it. All the way from making unwelcome sexual comments to women on the street to participating in gang rape – and everything in between. What's more, the vast majority of men who physically or sexually harass or assault women have never been caught or held accountable for their actions – according to virtually all credible law enforcement officials and academic researchers. Naturally, few of those who have abused women will be eager to have the spotlight turned onto men. But even men who have never knowingly harmed women sometimes feel uneasy about all of this. Long before #MeToo unleashed a newfound boldness among women – especially young women – to speak their truth and vocalize their rage, many men who understood that violence against women occurs on a continuum were aware that they participated in parts of male culture that contribute to misogyny and sexual exploitation.

But here's the thing: men don't have to be free of any whiff of sexism in order to speak out about it. They don't need to be ideologically pure and untainted. Few men would ever break their silence with a standard set that high. They do have to be willing to be introspective and self-reflective to a certain degree, and then do something to work for gender equity and against gender violence. And it's not just me – or other anti-sexist men – that say this. Over the years I have worked with countless women across the ethnic/racial spectrum – educators, advocates, movement leaders – who are committed to helping women and girls, and stopping the harm men do to them, but nonetheless have compassion for men and a welcoming spirit toward collaborating with them. One such woman is Esta Soler, the founder of Futures Without Violence, a San Francisco-based organization with a big footprint in the movement against gender-based violence. She coined a phrase that I use all the time: 'We need to invite men into the conversation, not indict them as potential rapists and abusers.'

4. Advocate for 'call in' versus 'call out' culture

Gender violence is an unpleasant topic. People who work with victims and survivors, as well as those who work with abusers, are often exposed to the ugly underside of human beings and the pain and suffering they are capable of inflicting on their fellow humans. And there is surely a place for calling out and condemning bad behaviour – and, when necessary, punishing people for doing harm. But when it comes to prevention, and the urgent need to bring men more fully into the struggle to change the social norms that fuel misogyny, there are ways to frame the issue more positively than stereotypical lectures about men behaving badly. Don't get me wrong; those have their place too. But in the epic struggle against misogyny and men's violence against women, men can and should be called on to do and be better, and to rise – in the timeless words of Abraham Lincoln – to the better angels of their nature. I constantly challenge men and young men to be more than simply 'one of the guys', which takes absolutely nothing special. What takes something special, if you're a guy, is to turn to your friends and tell them you're not cool with their sexist attitudes or behaviours. That is much more impressive, and requires much more self-confidence and skill than merely going along to get along. The point is to give men something positive to strive for, rather than just a negative thing to avoid.

The Black feminist anti-violence educator and reproductive rights campaigner Loretta Ross teaches a version of this that she describes as 'call-in culture'. It's a response to the rise in recent years of call-out culture, where people are shamed publicly for unintentional microaggressions, such as accidentally misgendering someone, or making a remark that someone might consider misogynous or racist. According to *New York Times* writer Jessica Bennett, to whom Ross spoke for a widely shared article in 2020, 'calling in is like calling out, but done privately and with respect'. Ross describes it as 'a call out done with love'.

Bennett explains that calling in may mean sending someone a private message, calling them to discuss the matter, or simply taking a breath before commenting, screenshotting or demanding they 'do better' without explaining how. The idea is to appeal to people's desire to do the right thing. 'Calling out assumes the worst,' Bennett writes. 'Calling in involves conversation, compassion and context. It doesn't mean a person should ignore harm, slight or damage, but nor should she, he or they exaggerate it.'

Ross concurs. 'Every time somebody disagrees with me it's not "verbal violence". I'm not getting "re-raped". Overstatement of harm is not helpful when you're trying to create a culture of compassion.'

I've used the 'call in' concept to frame anti-sexist action as a positive challenge for men – especially young men. Instead of calling out men for the bad things they and other men have done to women, I urge them to be among the men in their generation who have the courage, strength and moral integrity to break the historic pattern and rise to the occasion. The title of this book, *Every Man*, is intended as a call to arms, as opposed to an allocation of blame. I don't mean to suggest that I'm advocating for a lack of accountability. But in some instances, a discreet suggestion to a young man that he needs to check his misogynous attitudes and behaviours, and a gentle push in the right direction, can be the first step in a transformative journey.

The Benefits are for Everyone

One of the biggest misconceptions about the movements against domestic abuse and sexual violence is that, because they were created largely by and for girls and women, they haven't done much for boys and men. In fact the women-led movements against gender violence have made enormous contributions toward improving the lives of boys and men. The most obvious way they've done that is by helping women. The overwhelming majority of boys and men have girls, women and non-binary people in their lives whom they love – and in many cases desperately depend upon (e.g. their mothers). Any efforts that improve the quality of life for those people help the boys and men who care about them – by definition. Here are two more important examples of how boys and men's lives have improved as a direct result of women-led movements against domestic abuse and sexual assault:

1. Boys who live with domestic abuse

According to Women's Aid, one in seven children under the age of eighteen will have lived with domestic abuse at some point in their childhood. One in seven! And of course, the category of 'children' includes boys. Think about all the boys who are traumatized by what an adult man – their father, stepfather or mother's boyfriend – does to their mother. (Adult women and non-binary people can also be abusive.) Boys who grow up experiencing the trauma of domestic abuse may suffer lifelong effects on their physical, emotional and mental health, and be at greater risk of behavioural problems that include aggressive and violent acting-out. This is one of the reasons why juvenile justice programmes, jails, and prisons are filled with men whose life histories include traumatic family backgrounds.

One of the key factors that contribute to violence done

by men is violence done *to* them as boys – especially in childhood and early adolescence, and often in families. These abuse histories should never be used as excuses for later abusive behaviour, but they surely need to be part of the discussion in the search for solutions. The effects of childhood trauma can continue throughout the life cycle, as boys become men and carry their unresolved childhood trauma into adult relationships. There are countless adult men who are 'walking wounded' as the result of violence they suffered as children. The good news is that there has been outstanding progress in this area. A key insight from the domestic abuse movement is now enshrined in law: the UK's Domestic Abuse Act of 2021 makes clear that 'children who see or hear or experience the effects of domestic abuse involving someone with parental responsibility for them (either the victim or the perpetrator) are themselves victims of domestic abuse.'

2. Boys and men as sexual abuse survivors

According to the Centre of Expertise on Child Sexual Abuse, 15 per cent of girls and 5 per cent of boys in England and Wales experience sexual abuse before the age of sixteen. Children with physical and cognitive disabilities are twice as likely to be assaulted. The vast majority of perpetrators are male; in 2019/2020, men comprised 99 per cent of the people prosecuted for child sexual abuse.

Over the past couple of decades, public awareness about the sexual abuse of boys has increased dramatically, as have services for child, adolescent and adult survivors. The internalized shame that male survivors carry is still a serious impediment to progress – because unfortunately the tired old belief that a 'real man' is supposed to be invulnerable and able to protect himself still carries weight. And despite progress on LGBTQ issues, homophobia continues to play a role in keeping boys and men from coming forward and accessing services. Nonetheless, since the 1990s, numerous young and older men from diverse communities have broken the historic silence in male culture about these crimes.

A key driver of change was the stunning sexual abuse scandal in the Catholic Church that erupted in my home city of Boston in the early twenty-first century, and spread globally to religious institutions and other bastions of traditional patriarchal power. What is the connection between these momentous developments and the women-led movements against child sexual abuse? The women in these movements were at the forefront of calling public attention to boys' experience of sexual victimization – in the 1970s! The courageous male survivors who have started advocacy organizations and raised public awareness in recent decades about the boys who were traumatized by sexually abusive adults and older adolescents have been standing on the shoulders of the trailblazing women who created the cultural space for this difficult and transformative work.

Masculinities

Violence against women is a men's issue, but which men are we talking about? The category of people who identify as men is vast and highly variable. Men occupy many levels of power and privilege based on their socio-economic status, education, caste, race and religion, and whether they're locally born or first-generation immigrants. They can be straight, gay, heteronormative, trans. And they're not all created equal. Some men belong to groups that are culturally dominant; others represent more marginalized communities or identities. As a result, it's not fair – or particularly useful – to make sweeping statements about 'men' without accounting for the many power differentials between and among them. That's why sociologists in the twenty-first century increasingly use the term 'masculinities' – and why I use it in my writing.

In gender violence prevention work, it's especially necessary to acknowledge ethnic/racial nuances and complexities because one-size-fits-all solutions simply don't work. The need to apply a culturally sophisticated approach is perhaps most pronounced on issues of crime and policing, and whether and how the state intervenes in cases of domestic abuse and sexual assault. As far back as the 1970s, Black feminists in the US and UK worried about the disparate impact that criminal-justice-oriented responses to gender violence perpetration would have on communities of colour. Men of colour are much more likely to be arrested and incarcerated than white men, which often causes long-term negative effects on the people around them, including children, and cascading effects in the community. A history of mistrust between various ethnic groups and the police means that women in those groups who are victims of men's violence are less likely to report the crimes, and less likely to access domestic abuse and sexual assault survivor services. In addition, women who are migrants and refugees often feel pressure to protect the community – and sometimes their or the man's immigration status – by not disclosing the abuse to the authorities. Abusive immigrant men can deliberately use immigration status as a tactic to pressure their wives or girlfriends into remaining silent.

Ideas about gender, sex and power vary greatly from one culture to the next. What might be considered appropriate 'masculine' behaviour in one might be regarded as inappropriate or even abusive in another. Who is authorized to make determinations about what is or is not culturally accepted? And to what extent do people have to stay within their own group when they're critiquing men's beliefs or behaviours? In diverse societies like the UK and other European countries, tensions over issues like so-called honour killings, female genital mutilation and forced marriage call into question the balance governments must strike between multicultural sensitivities and more secular understandings of human rights and gender equality.

Men of colour are some of the most committed and effective anti-sexist male leaders around the world, whether in the UK, in the US, or throughout Africa, Asia and elsewhere. I've had the great privilege of facilitating or co-facilitating many gender violence prevention leadership trainings with men of colour, including indigenous male leaders in Australia, Hawai'i and across North America. At the beginning of those gatherings, I always make sure to acknowledge the obvious: I'm a white man from a wealthy and powerful country talking about re-visioning 'manhood' with men whose lived experiences of racism, colonial oppression and marginality I can never fully understand. At the same time, I make it clear that I won't accept the argument – and nor should anyone – that men's subordination and abuse of women is beyond reproach or criticism because 'that's how we do it in my culture', whatever culture that might happen to be. The great Nigerian feminist author Chimamanda Ngozi Adichie has a powerful rejoinder for that rationalization. 'Culture is constantly changing,' she writes. 'I have beautiful twin nieces who are fifteen. If they had been born a hundred years ago, they would have been taken away and killed. Because a hundred years ago, Igbo culture considered the birth of twins to be an evil omen. Today that practice is unimaginable to all Igbo people.'

Though it is now highly contested by modern global feminism, a deeply rooted belief in Western (and other) cultures is that men have a 'natural' or God-given right to control their girlfriends and wives. The widespread persistence of that belief is a key reason why domestic abuse rates remain so high around the world. Men who abuse their partners often describe this right in terms of the 'respect' they are owed, sometimes based on extreme patriarchal religious teaching or long-standing cultural practice. These larger systemic forces not only affect how men see themselves, they also shape the range of socially acceptable behaviours within which others can reasonably act. The same traditionalist beliefs that provide a (flawed) rationale for abuse can help to silence the abuser's friends and colleagues, who might not feel authorized to intervene, because that would be intruding on another man's 'private' family matters.

Social class and socioeconomic status also bear on the ways in which men act – and whether or not they're likely to be held accountable for misogynous abuse. For example, from the earliest days of the movement against domestic abuse, one of the most persistent cultural stereotypes has been that abusers are mainly men from poor and working-class backgrounds. It's a myth, of course, that upper-middle-class and wealthy men aren't part of the problem. But their abuse of women can sometimes be more effectively hidden. Abusive men with financial resources or social status can privately exert forms of 'coercive control' through financial abuse or emotional manipulation, and never even resort to using or threatening physical force. When they do assault their girlfriends or wives, some of these men are more adept at covering it up than men with lesser means, who along with their female partners are also more likely – for other reasons – to come into contact with the police and other agents of state authority.

How You Can Make a Difference

Part of the intent behind framing gender violence as a men's issue is that it sends a message to individual men that it's their responsibility *as a man* to deal with it, regardless of whether or not that causes discomfort. The goal is to make it normal and natural for men to engage with this topic, whether as part of a group of friends playing video games or sitting around a poker table, at work on the shop floor or in a corporate boardroom, or on the public stage. The first step might

---

simply be to bring up the subject in a conversation. Perhaps you can tell them you've recently been introduced to a new perspective, and it makes a lot of sense.

It doesn't make a man 'soft' or a 'beta' to point out and criticize misogyny, or to interrupt other men's sexism; quite the contrary, it often takes more guts and self-confidence to do so. Unquestionably, many men – including those in positions of leadership – are uncomfortable or inarticulate when talking about gender issues, just as many white people fear 'saying something wrong' when discussing race, particularly in the presence of people of colour. But just because it's sometimes difficult or awkward is never a good excuse for inaction, especially when it comes to men who are leaders – or aspire to be leaders. Over the years I have worked with countless men – including already powerful and influential men in the business, sports and military worlds – who for whatever reason have never been pushed to use their voice on the issue of gender violence prevention. In my experience, the first thing they need to hear is that men like them have a crucial role to play. Many men have heard this from women, but rarely from other men. That has its own special power, because when men see other men take a stand against misogyny and sexism, it helps them take more risks to do so themselves.

2. Blaming Victims, Chasing Monsters

'The most rage-provoking element of being a
female is the gaslighting that happens. For
centuries we've just been expected to absorb male
behaviour silently . . . When we, in our enlightened
state, in our emboldened state, now respond to bad
male behaviour . . . that response is treated like the
offence itself . . . I have no right to respond or I'm
crazy. I have no right to respond or I'm angry. I
have no right to respond or I'm out of line.'

— Taylor Swift

'Nothing is easier than to denounce the evildoer;
nothing is more difficult than to understand him.'

— Fyodor Dostoevsky, *Crime and Punishment*

Introspection isn't easy. That's as true for entire societies
as it is for individuals, which is why the paradigm shift
described in the previous chapter is such a challenge. I
wrote this book – and you're reading it – because there
is so much more we can all do – especially men – to
diminish the prevalence of gender-based violence
against women and girls all over the world. But in order
to do that we must first identify the ways in which the
dominant culture avoids accountability, and thereby

insulates itself from having to make necessary changes to the status quo. The two areas I want to highlight are 1) the time-tested tactic of blaming the victim, and 2) the popular framing of abusers as atypical and deviant monsters, rather than otherwise 'normal' guys who are products of our societies and thus in some way a reflection of all of us.

Victim-Blaming

Reframing gender violence as a men's issue is easier said than done, because it's very difficult to challenge the status quo. One key obstacle to change is the resistance women face when they try to hold men and male-dominated institutions accountable for abuse. They're often told what *they* need to do differently. This was on stark display in the aftermath of Sarah Everard's murder, when women were instructed to flag down a bus if they didn't feel safe, or ask to see a policeman's badge if he approached them. Despite the considerable outrage this prompted, it's understandable why women continue to hear this sort of advice. After all, holding men accountable – either as individuals or as a group – is more confrontational and can cause more drama. It also implicitly – and sometimes explicitly – shines a critical spotlight on the society that created them. This can be hard for people to hear, regardless of their gender: if it takes a village to raise a child, it also takes a village to raise a rapist. That implicates everyone – including good men. Blaming victims is a much easier proposition.

The classic definition of victim-blaming is when you shift accountability from the person causing harm to the person who has been injured. This is precisely what happens when you describe gender violence as a 'women's issue'; it becomes something that women – not men – are forced to deal with. The practice of blaming women for what men do to them is one of the oldest stories of humanity. What's new is that feminism has profoundly altered the consciousness of women over the past half-century. What was once seen as radical – that *women* are not responsible for *men's* violence – now seems common-sensical, at least to millions of women of all ethnic/racial backgrounds who reject the sort of conventional victim-blaming that held sway for thousands of years, and was a key factor in maintaining women's subordinate status. Younger women especially have been pushing back. Over the past decade or so they have begun to change the narrative about accountability, largely through the use of social media and other tools of digital technology that were unavailable to previous generations. One can see examples of this push-back all around – Instagram and Snapchat posts that contain pithy quotes like 'Don't tell women what to wear, tell men not to rape'. Signs at rallies that say 'Blame rapists not victims' and 'Don't get Raped', except the word 'get' is crossed out, along with the 'd' in 'raped'.

Blaming victims for their plight is hardly unique to gender violence; for those in a state of denial, it is often the go-to explanation for societal problems. It's especially popular with the powerful, or anyone who has a stake in defending established interests or social hierarchies. If the problem is that individuals bring misfortune on themselves, the solution is simple: fix or improve them. There is no need to hold the powerful to account, and ultimately no real need to change the status quo. That is why members of the prosperous classes often blame the character of the poor for their own poverty, or racist whites claim that racial inequality stems from cultural deficiencies in communities of colour. As long as the spotlight remains fixed on the victims, light can't shine on those who are actually responsible for the problem.

But blaming victims never solves anything. The poor can't end poverty, and if people of colour could put an end to racism, they surely would have long ago. In the same vein, rape and domestic abuse will not cease to exist when women manage to do a better job of avoiding them. They will end when our societies stop producing boys and men who think they have the right – for whatever reason – to dominate, control, coerce and violate women, other men, or anyone else. They will end when the people around those abusers make it clear that their behaviour is not just illegal or against the rules, but is also socially unacceptable. And they will end when we find effective and sustainable ways to hold abusers accountable – not their victims.

The Lowest-Hanging Fruit

The idea that the responsibility for acts of abuse should be placed squarely on the shoulders of abusers, and not on victims, represents a reversal of the ancient belief in Western and other world cultures that women bring men's abuse on themselves, either by their actions or by their shortcomings. For millennia this deeply misogynous belief served to absolve both male-dominated societies and individual men of their responsibility for doing grave harm to women, and very often shielded them from legal or even social accountability. Credit for the recent momentous reversal goes to the women-led movements against sexual and domestic violence that have transformed the social landscape over the past fifty years. Prior to the second half of the twentieth century, it was common to hear women who were sexually assaulted publicly chastised for 'leading men on' or 'putting themselves' in situations where they were especially vulnerable.

To be sure, those sorts of victim-blaming statements are still heard today, but due to a combination of feminist cultural influence and technological progress, a vociferous counterargument stands at the ready. Since even before #MeToo, young women on social media have been regularly circulating posts that critique victim-blaming statements in media accounts of sexual assaults or domestic violence incidents. Typically the poster expresses a mixture of frustration and outrage that, well into the twenty-first century, women – in the UK, Europe, the US, India, and all across the world – are still frequently blamed for what men do to them. And yet despite considerable progress in this area, some women continue to internalize this cultural bias and blame themselves for a man's actions. This makes it even less likely that they will come forward and try to hold perpetrators accountable – which is one of the reasons why victim-blaming plays such a powerful role in keeping the status quo intact.

Victim-blaming is also common because it is the

lowest-hanging fruit when it comes to addressing the reality of abuse. It asks the least of people. It ruffles the fewest feathers. This is because – in a nutshell – it is more difficult to hold a person or an institution accountable for their entitled or abusive behaviour than it is to blame someone for allowing themselves to be abused. On an interpersonal level, confronting a physically or sexually abusive man can be intimidating and scary for his family members, friends or colleagues, if not downright physically risky. After all, if you're trying to hold them accountable for committing violence, in some cases you might worry that they're capable of using violence against . . . you. Even if that is very unlikely, holding a perpetrator of abuse accountable – or attempting to do so – can be an enormously awkward and stressful undertaking. Your intervention might not be welcome in the slightest. It is thus much easier to avoid that stress and instead focus on the victim – arguably the least powerful person in the situation. If you or others make it about them, about something they did to bring it on themselves, you need not worry about having to face the wrath of the abuser.

You can see these dynamics play out in peer cultures when someone in the group reports that someone else in the group sexually assaulted her/him/them. Since everyone in the group knows both parties, the allegation forces people to think about what they should do. Take the example of an extended friendship group of university students. Before any legal or campus judicial proceeding arrives at a firm decision about the veracity of the claim or the disposition of the case, each student in the group needs to decide whether to believe or support either party. If they choose to take the side of the reported victim and profess belief in her version of events, they need to come to terms with the idea that their other friend has likely committed sexual assault. This can present an ethical dilemma, because if they don't say or do anything to express disapproval of that person's alleged behaviour, they might in some sense be guilty of at best minimizing the actions of, or at worst colluding with, the alleged rapist. Can they continue to be friends with someone who might have committed rape? What do they say to him? And if they don't make it clear to him that they disapprove of what he is alleged to have done, what does that say about them?

All of this can be quite stressful. If, however, they focus on the actions of the reported victim, on *her* supposed responsibility for the incident in question, they can sidestep all those awkward conversations. Rather than risk a confrontation with the alleged perpetrator, it is much easier to take the position that it was something *she* did that caused things to go wrong – and then, perhaps, support her in figuring out ways to cope with it.

Victim-blaming does more than merely shift account-ability off the one who caused harm. It also absolves the culture that produced him. Perpetrators of sexist abuse don't emerge mysteriously out of the primordial swamp; they are products of their society. They are typically 'normal' men in most measurable ways. In a sense, then, society shares some responsibility for socializing them, and for creating and perpetuating the beliefs and norms that often underlie the abuse. The problem is that if the values and practices of the larger society are implicated in the abuses committed by some of its members, there is blame to go around, because everyone – to a greater or lesser extent – plays a part in maintaining the social order.

For men especially, this line of reasoning forces a kind of reckoning. If men's violence against women is less a problem of individual pathology than a societal or cultural problem that manifests itself in the behaviour of individuals, men need to ask themselves what they are doing, through their actions or inaction, that contributes to ongoing suffering and tragedy. This sort of introspection can be discomfiting, because many non-violent, good men – if they are honest with themselves – know they are at least part of the problem. Furthermore, they know that in order to no longer be part of the problem, they'll need to make some changes. This, in turn, entails possibly giving up some things they might enjoy. For example, their participation in certain parts of lad or bro culture that give them feelings of pleasure and camaraderie with other men, but which are particularly misogynous.

Victim-blaming makes all of this hand-wringing unnecessary. When the focus is on the ways in which women bring harassment or abuse on themselves, men can evade introspection entirely – as well as avoid having to make the difficult changes it often compels.

Victim-Blaming Undermines Accountability for Perpetrators

In 1989, the American researcher Jennifer Freyd coined a term to describe something domestic abuse advocates had long observed in the courtroom behaviour of men charged with abuse. It's a tactic these men use to manipulate the court proceeding in their favour that she called DARVO: Deny, Attack, and Reverse Victim and Offender. The idea is to refute a woman's claim that the man abused her not only by denying the allegation, but by accusing her of being the true offender.

This is what happens on a broader scale when we call men's violence against women a 'women's issue'. The reversal shifts accountability away from the men who commit the violence and puts it onto women. It's about *her*. There's something wrong with *her*. This linguistic sleight-of-hand accomplishes a great deal: mainly, it prevents us from asking the kinds of questions we need to be asking if we want the violence to stop – questions that should be directed to abusive men.

Instead of asking why women stay with men who abuse them, we need to ask: why do men physically and emotionally abuse their girlfriends and wives? Instead of asking women why they put themselves in a position to be sexually assaulted, we should be asking men: why did you sexually assault a woman? In some cases, their answers can be extraordinarily revealing; many men who commit sexual assault have so internalized misogynous cultural beliefs about men's sexual entitlement and control over women that they don't see themselves as having done anything wrong. But generally we don't ask men these sorts of questions. Instead, we expend disproportionate energy on debates about what women do to 'make' themselves vulnerable.

There are circumstances in which calling gender violence

a 'women's issue' can be effective and even necessary; for example, if the ultimate goal is to muster support and funding for survivor services. But if the goal is prevention, anything that reduces accountability for men who use violence – or the culture that produces them – merely serves to perpetuate the problem.

Chasing Monsters

When we encounter abusive men, we often wonder: *What went wrong with him? What could have happened in his life to make him like that? Could he be mentally unwell? Maybe he's just a horrible person. What a monster!* But it is both misguided and unhelpful to think in cinematic terms about men who use violence as 'lone wolves' or monstrous individuals that crawl out of the swamp, come into town and do their nasty business, and then retreat into the darkness. It might be slightly comforting to think about them this way, because at least then the danger takes the classic form of an outside 'other'. But the truth is that most women who are assaulted by men are victimized by men they know – fathers, brothers, husbands, boyfriends. These are not random acts by twisted strangers, but part of a much larger system of gender inequality that is maintained by dynamics of power, control and entitlement, and infuses relationships in every stratum of society.

Another way to put this is that seemingly *personal* acts serve a *political* function. This was one of the most important – and controversial – insights in the bestselling feminist classic *Against Our Will: Men, Women and Rape*, written by the journalist and feminist activist Susan Brown-miller a half-century ago. Brownmiller shocked the world with her statement that 'rape is nothing more or less than a conscious process of intimidation by which *all* men keep *all* women in a state of fear.' She provided meticulous documentation of how pervasive rape has been for millennia, and demonstrated that what we now call 'rape-supportive' attitudes have long served to rationalize, legitimize and sometimes even encourage it. This forced a cultural reckoning when it came to the misguided idea that rapists are antisocial deviants and outliers. Brownmiller was making the powerful case that rape is a *political* act. Thus the pervasive problems of sexual violence and domestic abuse will be solved only by transforming underlying inequalities and the belief systems that sustain them – not by running from one broken man to the next and trying to figure out what went wrong.

Alas, the sweeping language Brownmiller used (i.e. *all* men, *all* women) was bound to provoke a backlash. Indeed, at the time it ignited a pre-social-media version of #NotAllMen. Then as now, some men – not all men! – find this entire line of reasoning uncomfortable and unwelcome, because it suggests that men who personally don't hurt women are nonetheless partially responsible for those who do. This resistance was evident in the resurgence of the trending #NotAllMen hashtag after women's fury boiled over following the murder of Sarah Everard.

Let me be clear: I think the #NotAllMen response was wrong-headed and counterproductive; I regularly advise men who want to be supportive to suppress the impulse to say such things. But I get the impulse. Who wants to be blamed for something you didn't do? Still, these men are a little late to the dance. Men have been expressing that sentiment – in one iteration or another – for centuries: *I'm not some sociopathic rapist. I'm a good guy. Don't paint all men with the same brush. It's not my fault that some guys are dicks.* The trouble with this argument is the logic is flawed, because it fails to grapple with the many ways in which men who don't physically or sexually assault women themselves nonetheless help to perpetuate the misogynous attitudes and social norms that underlie abusive behaviours by other men.

Along these lines, it's always important to keep in mind that the typical man who physically abuses, sexually harasses or sexually assaults women is not a sick or deviant person. Those individuals do exist. We've all seen their mugshots and gasped at their dishevelled and menacing appearance. But the average man who hurts women is not like that. He's disturbingly normal. You can't tell what he's done by the way he looks, what ethnic or racial group he belongs to, or how well he does his job. Indeed, there might be people in his professional or personal life with whom he has respectful relationships, or who might even find him charming. This makes women uncomfortable, of course, because whom can you trust? But it's also unsettling for many men – and not only because it places them under perpetual suspicion. I think many of them would prefer the stereotypical man who harms his partner to be some kind of monster, because then they could easily disidentify with him. *That guy's whack, evil, twisted. I'm nothing like him.* Just like victim-blaming, labelling individual perpetrators as monsters helps men evade responsibility for any sexist harms they might have contributed to or caused.

Racism operates here in a similar fashion. Some white people – not all white people – tend to blame the racialized other as the source of the problem. *It's* those *kinds of men who treat women poorly. It's part of their culture.* Not only does this sort of crude stereotyping rationalize racial or ethnic insensitivity or outright racism; it also serves to prevent critical self-reflection in white-majority communities with high rates of gender-based violence by deflecting blame elsewhere.

So it is with the caricature of men who use violence in their relationships as troubled, hot-headed brutes. Some men do commit monstrous acts. And it should go without saying that abuse is *never* justified. But, in reality, men who act abusively are not monsters. One of the key insights we've gained from people who work with men who use violence is that abusive men typically have a lot more in common with men who don't abuse than people might think. All men are subject to the influence of belief systems and cultural messages about what it means to be a man, especially with regard to their role in the family, and their relationship to women and children. Of course, most men don't interpret the meanings of those messages to endorse or justify sexist bullying or coercive behaviour. But consider the fact that 'risk factors' for domestic abuse perpetration include things like violence-supportive peer cultures, 'hostile sexist' attitudes, and rigid adherence to traditional gender norms – all of which, sadly, are still prevalent in key parts of mainstream culture.

Which brings us to this: if men who abuse women are in many other respects quite normal, isn't part of the solution to examine – and change – the underlying norms that contribute to the problem? And to that end, isn't it reasonable to ask non-abusive men to at least pause and reflect on the ways in which they might help to perpetuate those norms – even if they would never consciously or intentionally engage in sexist abuse themselves? Granted, many men find this entire exercise discomfiting and burdensome, which is why the idea that 'monsters' are wreaking havoc is oddly reassuring, even if it is highly misleading. *I'm not like those guys. I would never do those things.*

Men who work as facilitators in court-mandated programmes with men who have abused women often tell a revealing story about their first days on the job. Once they met and began to speak with the men, they realized that, far from the stereotype of one-dimensional ogres, many of them sounded perfectly ordinary. Many of them had good jobs and careers; many were fathers. What's more, the facilitators could see that in some cases they had more in common with the clients than they had anticipated – even some of their subtly sexist attitudes. That didn't mean they condoned the men's abusive behaviour, but it did mean they couldn't as easily distance themselves from it, either. After all, they grew up in the same time and place, went to the same schools, consumed the same media, and were socialized with the same misogynous cultural scripts about masculine entitlement and feminine subservience.

This is not to suggest that all men have the heart of a misogynist abuser hidden under a façade of feminist-conscious respectability. But obviously it can be disturbing to realize that many men who hurt women are otherwise regular guys. It would be so much easier if they weren't!

But true wisdom for men begins when we allow ourselves to be introspective and realize that it's not always about the *other*. Sometimes it's about us.

Unfortunately, many men's discomfort with this realization explains why they are also turned off by the feminist concept of 'rape culture'. They take it personally; it hits way too close to home. It's much easier to think about rapists the old-fashioned way – as deranged sociopaths or malevolent strangers lurking in the bushes waiting to pounce on their innocent and unsuspecting victims. That happens, but the vast majority of men who sexually abuse women know their victims – and vice versa. They're often family members, friends or exes. What's more, many of the men who do this to women don't even think they've done anything wrong. They're just doing what men do – or feel *entitled* to do. That is why so much anti-rape education over the past forty years has sought to debunk self-justifying rape myths – *he couldn't control his urges, she was asking for it, it can't be rape if she doesn't have physical bruises* – and replace those myths with facts. When prevalent rape myths go uncontested, some young men can delude themselves into believing that their aggressive actions are defensible, if not perfectly reasonable.

Challenging those myths has always been difficult. But today it's even more so, due to the proliferation of sexualized misogyny in pornography, along with the growth of the online men's rights movement that has broken out of its cloistered bubble and permeated mainstream spaces like YouTube and TikTok. Laura Bates, founder of the Everyday Sexism Project, says that a small but significant number of the boys she speaks to are deeply immersed in manosphere message boards. But the majority are not looking for this material – or even aware of it. Instead, she explains, the ideas come to them filtered through anonymous accounts and meme factories.

These are the boys and men – and there are many millions of them – who have grown up immersed in online worlds in which expressions of hostile sexism are pervasive, and whose sexual socialization has been driven by the aggressively anti-woman animus embedded in contemporary heterosexual porn. They have thus been groomed to fall deeper into the angry, misogynous world of online manfluencers like Andrew Tate and his growing cadre of imitators. In the next chapter, we'll take a closer look at some of the ways in which these cultural forces shape both individual behaviour and group norms.

How You Can Make a Difference

The impulse to blame victims and describe abusers as 'monsters' grows out of an understandable desire to look away from unpleasant realities and avoid uncomfortable truths. How can we counteract that impulse? An important first step is simply to name it. Call it out. Point out the ways in which it prevents us from getting to the roots of the problem. It's not easy to do, but the most straightforward solution is to tell the truth – or support those who do. Practically speaking, this means that people who are in a position to challenge victim-blaming and gaslighting statements about sexual assault and domestic abuse need to do so whenever possible – for example, by saying something like 'Hey, that's not fair!' when someone blames a woman for the harassment she gets from men for the clothing she wears. Because men – both as individuals and as a group – have historically used these tactics to evade accountability, it can be especially powerful when they're the ones who call them out.

3. Real Men and Rape Culture

'Rape culture is perpetuated through the use of misogynistic language, the objectification of women's bodies, the glamorization of sexual violence . . . It's so normalized to us that we make excuses about why we do what we do, or have done what we've done . . . the first step to the solution is recognizing that you can't heal what you can't reveal. And what we need to reveal and be morally honest about as men is that a lot of us were raised on rape culture.'

— Charlamagne Tha God

'[Boys] are bombarded with dangerous imagery, song lyrics, peer pressure, and often quite damaging/violent/entirely-intimacy-free pornography, all of which is sold to them as a glamorous and realistic norm.'

— Jameela Jamil

When I was in my twenties, after reading as much as I could, I reached the same conclusion that so many others have reached: men's violence against women – in all of its manifestations along a wide continuum of behaviours – is an inevitable consequence of the ways in which we socialize boys in a patriarchal culture, and more broadly of how we define what it means to be a man. It is not a 'natural' phenomenon, but rather the product of a set of gendered practices that grow out of – and reinforce – traditional hierarchies of gender and power. Gender is one of the chief organizing principles in every society, and the hierarchy that has evolved over thousands of years in the vast majority of them has put men *as a group* in a dominant position over women, and some men in positions of dominance over other men. That is what feminists mean when they use the word 'patriarchy', which Greta Gerwig and her collaborators satirized so brilliantly in the *Barbie* movie.

While patriarchy is a system that oppresses women first and foremost, it also has myriad negative effects on non-binary people – and on men. But not all men equally! Differences in power and privilege between and among men based on sexuality, class, race, ethnicity, religion, etc. need to be acknowledged – and accounted for. Moreover, contrary to the simple-minded criticism that feminism is anti-male, my initial motivation as a university student to give feminist ideas and analyses a fair hearing was curiosity and enlightened self-interest, rather than broader concerns about gender inequality and social injustice. Mostly, I wanted to improve my life and my relationships. I knew instinctively that – as the storyline of Ken in the *Barbie* movie illustrates vividly – traditional gender and sexual norms shape men's lives every bit as much as they do the lives of women and non-binary people. And not always for the better.

Before I jumped into public anti-sexist advocacy, I did some research into the specific 'causes' of domestic and sexual violence. I was convinced – then as now – that male children are born as innocent and loving as female children. So how does a loving little boy grow into an angry and controlling man? What happens along the way? Theories abound from a range of academic disciplines. A quick Google search reveals no shortage of explanations, and the research to back them up.

But what rang true for me about the majority of men's violence and abuse toward women was the startling fact that most abusers are average guys. With rare exceptions, their violence is not genetically predetermined. Their antisocial inclinations and aggressive impulses are not hardwired. So what causes their abusive behaviour? We know that some abusers were abused themselves. But it's impossible to offer totalizing explanations. The culture plays a big role, too.

It's also crucial to emphasize that men's violence against women takes place on a continuum, ranging from acts of casual sexism all the way to gang rape and femicide. That's why, for many men, this is such a sensitive subject. It's not enough to focus on the men who commit the most egregious acts of physical and sexual abuse. We have to widen the aperture and look more broadly at the rest of us: the millions of men who have – unwittingly or not – engaged in behaviour that contributes to the continuum of harm. Which brings us to the topic of rape culture.

Rape Culture

The concept of rape culture emerged in the 1970s as a way to explain high rates of sexual violence around the world by demonstrating that these acts of violence were not isolated incidents, but the result of a climate of misogyny and sexism that normalized the harm and abuse of women. Rape and sexual assault are too shockingly common to describe them as the deeds of a few 'lone wolves' or 'monsters'. One in four women over the age of sixteen has been raped or sexually assaulted in England and Wales, and one in eighteen men. What does that tell us? Because men commit the overwhelming percentage of rape and sexual assault, regardless of the sex of the victim, a disturbingly high number of British men have committed rape and sexual assault, even accounting for the fact that some are multiple offenders. Why? Are human males hardwired to sexually violate women and non-binary people, as well as other men? Isn't this just another version of the old 'boys will be boys' rationalization? Isn't it more helpful to women, non-binary people *and* men to examine the ways in which harmful gender norms produce seemingly 'normal' men who commit sexual offences, and work toward changing them?

The ultimate goal of prevention is to shift the social and cultural norms that give rise to abuse. One way to do so is to encourage men to speak up and interrupt instances of sexism by other men in their sphere of influence – from the most egregious examples to the more subtle and nuanced. The idea is to expand the number of men who feel invested in becoming part of the change. In my talks and trainings, I use a visualization exercise with a large triangle as a way to conceptualize this, pictured opposite. Let's walk through it.

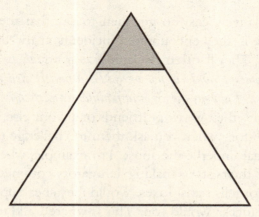

Fig. 1. A modified rape culture pyramid

Imagine that the triangle is a pyramid. The tip, which is shaded in, represents an incident of gender-based violence: a sexual assault, an act of domestic abuse or an instance of sexual harassment.

The base consists of misogynous comments, rape jokes, catcalls, anti-woman song lyrics, locker-room banter, and a range of other practices that help to normalize sexism, and thus to create the cultural conditions that support and even encourage incidents such as the one at the tip of the pyramid. It includes old media, such as the rampant sexual objectification of girls and women in advertising. It includes the ubiquitous and openly misogynous culture of porn. It also includes new-media phenomena such as social media, image-based sexual abuse, and the growing online manosphere, in which – often under the cloak of anonymity – men routinely issue venomous attacks on women for withholding sex from them, and rage against women (especially feminists) for allegedly ruining their lives.

It's relatively easy to get men to say that they would intervene if they encountered incidents at the tip of the pyramid. They'll often declare: *Sexual assault is a horrible crime. Domestic abuse is not okay. I'd definitely step in and do something if I saw my friends or acquaintances mistreating women* – whether it's their wives, girlfriends or anyone else. But it's a different story when you ask them to challenge the sexist beliefs that underlie the abuse. For example, when a male friend of theirs starts making derogatory comments about women, or tells sexist jokes. Would they speak up in those circumstances? Would you? This is where I and my fellow educators and trainers start to face pushback. *Really? This is taking things too far. I agree that we need to intervene when we see abuse. But you want me to tell people what they should and shouldn't laugh at? You're asking me to be the morality police!* In other words, when the focus turns to the base of the pyramid – i.e. the normalization and routinization of misogyny – consensus about the urgent need for action begins to erode. In my trainings, guys will sometimes even question whether various actions and practices in the base even qualify as abuses. *Lighten up!*

Misogynous lyrics in rock and rap songs have long been a source of controversy and debate – in both social networks and academic settings. Likewise, the topic of misogyny and comedy can generate especially spirited dialogue. Are jokes that demean women and women's sexuality – especially when told by men – really harmful? Or are people who are troubled by them just snowflakes that can't take a joke, or worse, don't understand the point of comedy, or even the principle of free speech? Of course, conversations about the base of the pyramid are bound to be contentious, because many men can get defensive and even feel attacked. And not without cause. Many of us *have* participated in sexist rituals – whether or not we intended to perpetuate a culture of misogyny, and whether or not we were even aware we were doing so at the time. Many of us have looked the other way when our friends or colleagues call women 'bitches' or 'hoes'. We've participated in a culture of casual sexual objectification and harassment in pubs and clubs. We've laughed at sexist jokes, sung along to misogynous songs, been turned on by degrading porn, paid for sex, gone to strip clubs with the guys. It's tough for many men to look at the base of the pyramid and not see some of their own behaviours, along with those of their mates.

That's what makes the concept of a 'rape culture' sound off-putting and extreme to a lot of men. They don't want to think of themselves as part of a system that does great harm to women and non-binary people, as well as men themselves. But if they want to actually do something to change the status quo, to reduce the outrageously high levels of gender-based violence and harassment in their society and others, they must be willing – at a minimum – to look in the mirror, and at least entertain the possibility that the foundation of these problems is located not at the tip of the pyramid, but at its base.

The problem, of course, is that we often find it much easier to focus on the pathologies and shortcomings of individuals than to analyse and critique broader societal norms. But focusing narrowly on individuals means that we can miss the larger picture. Individuals are products of social systems. And while each person has unique attributes, they are also profoundly shaped by factors like their time and place, the socioeconomics of their community and family, their ethnicity/racial identity, the social worlds they inhabit, the media they consume, and for our purposes here, how they 'do gender' – and whether it complies or clashes with the norms of their society.

We could just focus on 'point of attack' interventions and call it prevention, but, in reality, nothing much would change. Keep in mind that the vast majority of incidents of gender-based violence happen in private, so most of the time no one's even there to intervene. By contrast, most of what happens at the base of the pyramid takes place in peer cultures, online or in public. This means that, to a certain extent, we all play a role in either perpetuating or challenging norms. Throughout the course of this book, but especially chapter 6 on bystanders, I will explain how you can speak up, step in and interrupt misogynous behaviour from your friends, teammates, co-workers and family members, but for now I want to explore some of the ways in which misogynous beliefs and behaviours have been normalized at the base of the pyramid.

Learned vs Taught Behaviour

Where do these behaviours come from in the first place? Many people think that interpersonal violence is driven less by biological factors and more by psychological and sociological ones, and therefore it must somehow be the consequence of *learned* behaviour. This theory has merit, but I have never liked the term 'learned behaviour'. It's too passive. I'd rather call it *taught* behaviour. Boys and young men don't passively 'learn' things like how, when and where to use violence, or who to see as the appropriate targets of their aggression. They don't just 'learn' to sexually object-ify girls and women, treat them disrespectfully or feel justified in coercing and controlling them. Someone – or something – teaches them. Who or what teaches them? Parents and other adult caregivers obviously play a crucial role in the moral development and socialization of their children. But children are exposed to so many influences beyond their immediate family – their friends and peers, social media, films and other entertainment.

I decided to study media when I first went to graduate school in the early 1990s because I wanted to understand more about the ways in which men and masculinities were being portrayed, and what that might teach us about how boys and men are socialized to think about and use violence, including violence against women. At the time, the study of masculinities in media was in its infancy. Feminist theorists and media literacy educators had been studying images of women since the 1970s. They had pointed out, for example, that unnaturally thin and white standards of feminine beauty as represented in advertis-ing and other media helped produce widespread body image problems and eating disorders among girls and women. When I was beginning my violence prevention work, I set out to apply similar analytic tools to images and narratives about men.

I found it notable that in the stories we tell about men in Hollywood films, television, sports, song lyrics, video games, and advertising, the idea of being a 'real man' is too often equated narrowly – and often cartoonishly – with a man's willingness to use violence, not only to defend himself or his loved ones, but also to prove his ability to impose his will on rivals, or exact revenge against his enemies. For heterosexual men, this performance of masculinity often carries over into the enactment of dominance in sexual relations with women. Sexually, 'real men' are supposed to take what's theirs and always be the actor, never the acted-upon. That's the 'feminine' role. This broader exploration of the role of media narratives in defining what it means to be a 'real man' led me inevitably to look into porn and its effects, since porn is not only an influential and ubiquitous form of media but is also by far the world's most important instructional manual for male sexuality. Where schools have failed to teach sex education, porn has stepped in as a way to provide boys and young men with 'information' about how to have sex; about what is normal and expected of 'real men'. Today, it is simply inconceivable that we can have a thoughtful conversation about how to bring down the persistently high rates of sexual harassment, abuse and rape and not talk about the role of misogynous porn in shaping and distorting the sexual psyches of boys and men.

Men and Porn

A survey commissioned by the BBC in 2019 found that more than a third of UK women under the age of forty had experienced unwanted slapping, choking, gagging or spitting by their partners during 'consensual' sex. Put another way, millions of men in the UK have slapped, choked, gagged or spit on their reluctant girlfriends or wives during sex. Why have they done this? Is it because they've been led to believe that's the way men are supposed to behave during sex? If that's the case, where did they 'learn' such a thing? It's not really a great mystery. In an era of ubiquitous porn that has grown ever more misogynous and degrading over the past few decades, heterosexual men increasingly have been conditioned to identify the enactment of masculinity with sexualized dominance and control over women's bodies.

This porn – easily available on smartphones, and thus readily accessible to young and highly impressionable boys – provides a steady stream of visual narratives that normalizes men's callous and cruel sexual treatment of women. How does this consumption influence their attitudes, beliefs and behaviours toward women – in and out of the bedroom?

The BBC survey clearly demonstrates that consuming porn can inform how men treat their sexual partners in real life. And we're on new social terrain. University of Sydney senior lecturer Samuel Shpall calls the ubiquity of digital sex 'an astonishing historical departure'. Young men are 'experts about this topic in a way that nobody else is because they're kind of like the first generation that was literally raised on internet pornography. Their generation [is] in a completely different kind of moral development, in terms of how their sexual psyche is mediated by the awesome availability of pornographic material.' Many young men themselves recognize this is harmful. Shpall says that 'when a guy in a class says things like, "The vision of male sexuality that we grew up on is just toxic, right?" . . . there's a lot of nods.'

Since the 1970s, debates about the effects of heterosexual porn – and the relationship between porn and men's violence against women – have caused deep divisions within feminism. Over these few decades, the size and scope of the porn industry has reached new proportions. In 2019 alone, the popular website Pornhub had over 42 billion visits. And while the amount of porn being consumed has grown, the content itself has become more openly misogynous and brutal. One 2010 study showed that 88 per cent of scenes in a selection of popular porn videos contained physical aggression – primarily spanking, gagging and slapping. Almost half the scenes contained verbal aggression and degradation, primarily name-calling. Not surprisingly, the vast majority of this was men aggressing against and degrading women. And as if this weren't bad enough, the internet has made this porn more accessible to children. A 2023 Commonsense Media survey found that the average age at which kids were exposed to porn was twelve years old; 15 per cent first saw porn when they were ten years old or younger.

Evidence of the real-world harms of this exposure continues to grow. An alarming report released in 2024 by the National Police Chiefs' Council found that of 107,000 reports of sexual offences against children in England and Wales in 2022, 52 per cent of the offenders were also children, the vast majority of whom were boys. The NPCC lead for child protection Ian Critchley said that 'this is predominantly a gender-based crime of boys committing offences against girls . . . exacerbated by . . .

the ease with which violent pornography is accessible to boys, and, therefore, a perception that [what they see is normal] behaviour.' Numerous studies over the past several decades reveal evidence that exposure to or consumption of pornography is related to male sexual aggression against women. Studies from around the world show that porn use by teen boys is associated with sexual coercion, callousness, and dating violence. Australian sociologist Michael Flood summarizes the key research findings as follows: 'Exposure to porn increases rape myth acceptance, sexual callousness, and adversarial sexual beliefs. Exposure to violent porn also desensitizes them to sexual violence, and erodes their empathy with female rape victims.'

Then there's the topic of consent and how to understand and define it. Gender violence prevention educators spend a good portion of their limited classroom time with young people addressing the question of sexual consent – i.e. how it is legally defined? How can you be sure you have it? But it's a tough job, because many young people feel they have already 'learned' about consent, and they see a marked difference between what the textbook says and what they've already been 'taught'. It's not a big stretch to believe that young men for whom porn is their primary – or only – form of sex 'education' might believe that women often say 'no' when they mean 'yes', 'maybe' or 'try harder'. They might listen to Andrew Tate or other charismatic personalities on social media who insist that 'real men' get what they want. If boys have been regularly exposed to scenes where a woman initially says 'no' but this turns into an enthusiastic, screaming (fake) orgasm, is it a great leap to think they might feel justified and embold-ened to push past a sexual partner's reticence? Isn't it also possible to think that if he does eventually gain her compliance, it might reinforce the idea that this is the 'normal' way heterosexuals have sex, when it might actually be sexual assault or even rape?

The British-American feminist sociologist and author Gail Dines says in her public lectures that porn teaches girls to capitulate rather than consent. Along with other forms of cultural instruction, it trains them to be, in a sense, 'compliant victims'. When combined with the guidance boys and men receive to be sexually aggres-sive, this creates 'perfect storm' conditions to facilitate rape. Laura Bates says that when she visits schools, she frequently hears young people say that 'rape is a compli-ment, really' or 'crying is foreplay'. She recounts a story about a school she visited where they had had a rape case involving a fourteen-year-old boy. A teacher asked, 'Why didn't you stop when she was crying?' The boy looked at her, bewildered, and said, 'Because it's normal for girls to cry during sex.'

Porn also teaches heterosexual boys and young men that sex is something men do *to* women, and often violently. An analysis of porn titles by sociologist Fiona Vera-Gray and colleagues found that one in eight titles shown to first-time users on the first page of mainstream porn sites describes sexual activity that constitutes sexual violence. Depictions of sex in the universe created by the 'gonzo' porn on offer to heterosexual boys and young men almost never features reciprocal pleasure; women's sexual needs are barely worthy of mention. In fact, in pornland, men are conditioned to be turned on by women's discomfort – or worse. As the writer Lili Loofbourow puts it, we 'live in a culture that sees female pain as normal and male pleasure as a right'.

At the same time, the violent ways in which many men describe what they do to women through sex – or what they're *supposed* to do – is revealing and disturbing in light of how much violence women report they experience in the 'real world'. In her book *Boys & Sex: Young Men on Hookups, Love, Porn, Consent and Navigating the New Masculinity*, Peggy Orenstein describes a conversation with a group of (straight) high school boys in which they recount the ways they talk to each other about sex with girls. *I destroyed her. I ripped her up. Fucked her. Nailed her. Banged her. Pounded her. Slammed her.* You don't have to take any of this literally in order to see that this casual use of sexually violent language contributes to a belief system and way of thinking about sexual activity that has little to do with intimacy and connection – or anything even close to sexual freedom or liberation.

The Normalization of Sexualized Violence

For young heterosexual men, porn often functions as a how-to guide for sex, while for young women it can play the role of a grooming tool in which they start to see men's sexual violence as normative. What could go wrong? Perhaps the most alarming aspect of the normalization of sexualized violence is the way in which men 'choking' women is presented in porn as fun and sexy. Pornhub today features more than 10,000 #choking videos that get tens of millions of views, all freely available at the push of a button to anybody, regardless of age. Except it's not choking by any medical definition – it's strangulation. It's stunning that porn has helped to normalize and make 'sexy' a behaviour that domestic abuse professionals have increasingly recognized not only as an extreme form of men's power and control, but one that can have significant negative health effects – in addition to being a major homicide risk factor for women.

Feminist researchers have long observed that media socializes girls – especially heterosexual girls – to see their value in their looks and ability to attract men. Studies show that viewing porn takes them one step further: it is correlated with women feeling compelled to submit to sexually degrading and violent behaviours, in order to be visible and valued by men. Fiona Vera-Gray says many young women didn't realize, until they were much older, that they could say they didn't like having their hair pulled or being spat at, or being choked, because all the boys they were having sex with were doing it, and all the porn they were watching showed women getting pleasure from it. They thought there must be something wrong with them if they didn't like it.

At the same time, boys and young men can feel as if they should be aroused by sexual aggression – even if they don't feel comfortable with it – because it's presented in porn as masculine and normative to do so. 'Men don't have permission to opt out,' Vera-Gray says, because of the dominant (and misleading) narrative that all men use porn. One solution she offers: men need to talk to other men about porn. Over many years, my colleagues and I have conducted workshops with groups of young men on university campuses and in communities to do just that. We try to approach the issue from the angle of the social pressures many young men feel about their porn use. One way to open a conversation about this with a group of friends or in a classroom is to ask: 'Have you ever found yourself in a situation where you felt pressure to watch porn, or go to a strip club? Or to pretend that you were into it when you really weren't?'

A growing body of research on this subject has provided useful insight and helped educators and others develop general principles to guide conversations on porn, especially with young men. According to Michael Flood, these include addressing the powerful appeal of porn, destigmatizing masturbation, and avoiding the pathologizing of sexual interests or desires – even while trying to mobilize some young men's discomfort and guilt about the sexism in pornography.

Porn: A Public Health Crisis?

Gail Dines founded the US-based organization Culture Reframed in 2015 to redefine porn as the 'public health crisis of the Digital Age'. Since the 1990s, Dines has delivered hundreds of illustrated anti-porn lectures, many to large audiences of university students, healthcare professionals, child abuse prevention advocates and others, in packed halls, hotel ballrooms and conference centres. Her lectures feature dozens of disturbing images from mainstream and widely available porn, depicting men degrading women sexually, and they often provoke strong and visceral responses – and not just from women. 'Over the years I have come to understand how and why my presentation stirs up extreme emotions in men,' she writes in her book *Pornland: How Porn Has Hijacked Our Sexuality*. 'What I do in my presentations is take the very images that users have viewed privately and with pleasure, and I project them onto a screen in a public forum. In the decidedly nonsexual arena of a college auditorium, men are asked to think critically about what the images say about women, men, and sexuality. Stripped of an erection, men are invited to examine their porn use in a reflective manner while thinking about how images seep into their lives.'

Dines says that sometimes adult men – many of whom are liberal and progressive – are sceptical about a connection between porn and sexual violence. Above all, they want to know: 'Does it lead to rape?' She responds that a more subtle question would be: how does porn shape the culture and the men who use it? 'No anti-porn feminist I know has suggested that there is one image, or even a few, that could lead a non-rapist to rape; the argument, rather, is that taken together, pornographic images create a world that is at best inhospitable to women, and at worst dangerous to their physical and emotional well-being.'

What Dines and her colleagues are doing – along with a growing number of organizations in the US, UK, Europe, Australia and elsewhere – is laying out piles of evidence from public health experts, sexual health experts, paediatricians, adolescent psychologists, sociologists, neuroscientists, educators and researchers that misogynous porn is not harmless fantasy, but instead causes measurable harm not only to women, but also to men themselves. Dozens of studies over the past decade or more have shown that men's use of pornography can have seriously negative repercussions on their sexual health, including their ability to have positive sexual experiences with an intimate partner. There is also the matter of men's conscience. Robert Jensen, author of *Getting Off: Pornography and the End of Masculinity*, says that men who believe in the principles of equality, justice, fairness and mutual respect cannot patronize the sexual exploitation industries of stripping, prostitution and porn without violating the principles they claim to hold. Many men are deeply conflicted about the fact that our sexuality has been so fused to the objectification of women and the commodification of sex. We don't feel good about it. 'Much of the guilt and shame that many men report from using pornography', he writes, 'is a result not of religiosity or prudishness but the recognition that using objectified female bodies for pleasure – the essence of pornography – is at odds with who we want to be. We want to be fully human, and pornography makes that difficult, and we know it.'

The Manosphere

Misogynous porn depicts a steady stream of narratives that normalize men's callous and cruel sexual treatment of women. But if porn provides the visual storytelling, the online manosphere provides a complementary forum of websites, chat rooms and other social media platforms where men express and encourage unchecked resentment, hostility and anger toward women.

The misogynous manosphere has been growing and evolving since the birth of the internet. Laura Bates's 2020 book *Men Who Hate Women* details its rise from a collection of subcultures, including incels (or 'involuntarily celibate' men who blame women for their sexual failings), pickup artists and fathers' right groups who found a global online community of support and solidarity. In more recent years, social media has played its role in pushing the views of these men from the fringes into mainstream culture. Today, the manosphere is associated with online harassment, radicalization and the glorification of violence against women. Unfortunately, but not surprisingly, the reach of this volatile – and occasionally murderous – virtual community has been amplified by social media algorithms and weaponized by right-wing, anti-feminist populist movements in the UK, Europe, the US and elsewhere.

'Manfluencers' with particularly extreme opinions about women have found fame and fortune through the manosphere. But none has approached the popularity and reach of Andrew Tate, who has been called the 'King of Toxic Masculinity'. Tate is a former world champion kickboxer whose notoriety grew after he was kicked off the reality TV show *Big Brother* in the UK in 2016, when a video surfaced of him appearing to beat a woman with a belt. No criminal charges were filed; both Tate and the woman in the video claimed it was fully 'consensual'. The videos he puts out on social media feature him saying things like women belong at home, shouldn't drive and are men's property.

Tate has built a vast audience both because he is highly skilled at gaming social media algorithms, and because he has carefully cultivated his image as an 'alpha male' that young men can look to for guidance and inspiration. Before he was kicked off Twitter in 2017 after he claimed that rape victims must 'bear responsibility' for their attacks, his social media content had received approximately 11.6 billion views. He was reinstated when Elon Musk bought the company in 2022. Later that year, Tate was arrested with his brother, Tristan, and two others, for human trafficking and rape. According to the authorities in Romania, where he was arrested, 'The four suspects . . . appear to have created an organized crime group with the purpose of recruiting, housing and exploiting women by forcing them to create pornographic content meant to be seen on specialized websites for a cost.' Even after those charges were filed, Tate appeared on the *Piers Morgan Uncensored* show and other programmes, where his appearances attracted many millions of views, and where the hosts solicited his opinions on everything from the struggles of young men, to climate change, to Israel and Palestine.

Tate's popularity, especially with teenage boys, is undoubtedly due to his charisma and savvy at marketing his brand. He also conveys a compassionate, even paternal, concern for the well-being of boys and young men. He insists that he feels a deep sense of responsibility to them, and claims that he wants to help them succeed like he did: by working himself up from nothing to a situation in which he owns multiple homes, some of the most expensive cars and watches in the world, and sleeps with beautiful women. His message to young men is clear and consistent, but also cartoonishly hypermasculine and misogynous: if you want to succeed, you must take what you deserve as a man.

In one video, Tate complained that 'women are failing in their role', which he said should be to cook for a man and give birth to children. In an interview with a YouTuber, he said, 'I'm a realist and when you're a realist, you're sexist. There's no way you can be rooted in reality and not be sexist.' In a 2022 interview with Barstool Sports, Tate came very close to saying that if he was being a protector and financially 'responsible' for a woman he might be in a relationship with, she was in effect his property. Later he clarified, 'I'm not saying they're property. I am saying they are given to the man and belong to the man.' He said he dates women aged 18–19 because he can 'make an imprint' on them.

Tate's influence seemed to accelerate during the pandemic, when schools closed and boys were confined to their houses, and thus had more time to explore the internet and fewer opportunities to discuss what was normal and acceptable with their teachers and friends. Stories began to appear in national newspapers with headlines like 'Teachers Warn That Misogynist Andrew Tate Has "Radicalised" School-Age Boys'. It should be noted that some of his young male fans apparently take his pronouncements seriously; others think he's playing a character and it's all just an act. But regardless of his intent, Tate has clearly helped to normalize expressions of overt misogyny. By the end of the pandemic in 2022, a YouGov survey found that 26 per cent of men in the UK aged 18–29 who had heard of Tate agreed with his opinions on women, as did 28 per cent of men aged 30–39. This is especially concerning when you consider that his audience includes many millions of young men who have received a barrage of mixed messages over the past generation about what it means to be a man in a time of rapid social transformation.

Arguably Andrew Tate has done as much to rationalize and normalize misogyny as anyone in the world. But when an entrepreneur like Tate monetizes misogyny to become rich and famous, it tells us less about him and more about the lives and psyches of his fans. He understands that millions of young men are confused, frustrated and lonely. He didn't cause the disillusionment, but he's exploiting it for all it's worth. The lecturer and author Alice Evans explains it like this: Tate is 'not just an exogenous shock, single-handedly brainwashing innocent young men. Rather, he's surfing a wave of economic frustration, turbo-charged by corporate algorithms that fire up sensationalist content for clicks.'

For young heterosexual women, the negative consequences of Tate's popularity with men are obvious. These women will often find themselves partnered with men who believe – consciously or not – that men's emotional and sexual needs come first, and that women's most important role is to serve men. In an era where growing numbers of women are demanding equal treatment and respect for their basic human rights, this is a recipe for conflict. But the ideal of 'manhood' Tate promotes also harms boys and young men, because it teaches boys that selfish materialism, without regard for its human consequences, is a formula for success. It sets boys up for a lifetime of failure in intimate relationships and friendships with girls and women, for which they often blame the women, fuelling a vicious cycle. And it misleads boys into thinking that certain kinds of misogynous behaviour – such as harassment or coercive control – are 'normal', when they are in fact *criminal*.

How You Can Make a Difference

If you're a man, bring up the issue you have with porn with other men when you're in a position to do so. When someone says 'everyone watches porn', and you have chosen not to, consider saying so. Guys need to hear that it's okay not to participate in something many people are conflicted about – and not only if your objections are based on religious beliefs. Men in positions of influence with young men and boys – fathers, uncles, older brothers, mentors – have an especially critical role to play. Don't wait for them to ask questions; initiate the conversation yourself. A good opening is to tell them you're concerned about them because online porn is so harmful, not only to women but to young men themselves. Fortunately, there's a growing consciousness of this harm, along with an acknowledgement of the value in opening up lines of communication about this difficult and important subject.

Andrew Tate and his imitators draw much of their support from boys and young men who believe they're the only ones who care about men and their struggles. This belief is not only wrong, it's absurd. For example, since the 1970s, the multiracial, multi-ethnic pro-feminist men's movement has been devoted to improving virtually every aspect of men's lives, which includes men's health in all its dimensions: emotional, psychological, relational, physical and sexual. Obviously this movement still has a long way to go, but it has contributed to the transformation of old, tired and sometimes harmful expectations and norms about 'manhood'. Accordingly, one way to counteract the malign influence of Tate and the misogynous manosphere is to point people toward the countless websites, social media campaigns and grassroots initiatives generated by this movement, along with numerous articles, books, documentary films and TED talks that address 'men's issues' while simultaneously supporting women's rights and gender equity. A good place to start is chapter 8 of this book, and in the notes section and bibliography, where I outline some of these resources.

4. Pushback

One of the most powerful forces against progress in gender violence prevention is the defensiveness many men bring to this topic. And I get it – I can be as self-protective as the next guy. In the first chapter, I outlined some of the techniques I developed to counter this defensiveness by staying positive and appealing to men's desire to be helpful and socially responsible. I have written this chapter because sometimes staying positive is not enough. I am well aware that some people disagree with this book's central thesis: that violence against women is a men's issue. My goal is to provide readers with language they can use to rebut those arguments. But the barriers to progress are not just external, so in the second half of this chapter I will take a look at some of the internal processes in men's psyches that hold them back from being empowered agents of change.

How to Rebut Counterarguments

Some men might feel frustrated by the last chapter, or object to the term 'rape culture'. *They* would never rape someone. Listening to a song or watching some videos doesn't make *them* a bad person. As an educator who works to end men's violence against women, I have experienced all kinds of responses to the call for change. When

I was young I used to hear: *You don't really believe this stuff, do you? You're just sucking up to girls so you can get laid.* Today, the pushback I get is often angrier and nastier, and more likely to come from anonymous posters and commenters in response to my online content. But I don't usually take it personally.

Regardless of the source, the objections people raise are often highly predictable and tend to coalesce around a number of themes. You might even recognize some of them.

Not All Men

If violence against women is a men's issue, does that mean all men, or just the ones committing the violence? The reason why the #NotAllMen hashtag during #MeToo touched such a nerve – on all sides – is that it went right to the heart of how people see the problem. Is it about the indefensible behaviour of a small percentage of bad actors, or is the larger community somehow implicated? I've long known it's more about the latter than the former, but I did smile when I came across the #NotAllMen hashtag a few years ago. It reminded me of how I felt when I first learned about all of this when I was at university. I was part of an innovative peer health education programme that conducted workshops for students on issues of gender and sexuality. We used to do a 'fishbowl' exercise where one sex would sit as a group in the middle of the room, and the other would sit in a circle around them. (At the time, binary categories for sex and gender were largely unexamined.)

The students in the middle would have a conversation with each other, based on note cards the peer educator read aloud that contained things people had written anonymously in response to various prompts. Only when their time was up could those on the outside join the conversation, make comments and ask their own questions. Then the two groups would switch places. Perennially, the most popular prompt for the men said: 'If you could make a statement that all women would hear, what would it be?' Many of the men offered variations on a theme that resonated strongly with me: *Not all men are jerks. Lots of men love and respect women. Don't judge me by the behaviour of other men.*

Today, I regularly counsel men to avoid saying 'not all men' under any circumstances. Why? It sounds unnecessarily defensive. No one has said it is all men! Sometimes, the phrase can signal to women that your need to be seen as one of the 'good guys' takes priority over their expressed desire to have their experience with abusive men – or misogyny in general – acknowledged and validated. But #NotAllMen is also misguided because – once again – it individualizes a systemic problem. A man who says it probably figures that violence against women is not his problem if he doesn't engage in misogynous abuse himself. And he might be right – in a very narrow sense. Obviously not all men sexually or physically abuse women. In fact, many are horrified by that sort of behaviour and can't see themselves ever doing anything remotely like it. But how many men can say they don't contribute – in any way – to abuse-supportive beliefs? It's impossible to do this if one understands the idea that violence against women occurs on a continuum.

In an article about the overlaps in the misogynous language and sentiments espoused by incels and mainstream pornography entitled 'I Don't Hate All Women, Just Those Stuck-Up Bitches', University of Portsmouth senior lecturers Alessia Tranchese and Lisa Sugiura argue that it's a mistake to draw artificially clear distinctions between the 'crazy fringes' of misogyny and more mundane ideologies. 'The extreme/non-extreme dichotomy is misleading', they write, because this arbitrary division absolves the 'non-misogynistic' majority, which is allowed to reject extreme misogyny even as it preserves gender inequality through normalized practices such as the consumption of gonzo pornography that depicts hardcore, body-punishing sex in which women are demeaned and debased.

Whataboutism

In the current era of anti-feminist backlash, whenever someone calls attention to violence against women – especially on the internet – it's a pretty good bet they'll be met with a flurry of invective directed at them by an online mob of angry men. *You're overlooking male victims! What about all the men who are abused by women? Don't you know that men are the primary victims of violence?* This is classic whataboutery. Whether used by men's rights activists in the misogynous manosphere, or by ordinary guys with no conscious political agenda, it is a tactic of denial and deflection that is designed to delegitimize women's experiences and turn the spotlight back onto men. Not as perpetrators that should be held accountable, but as *victims* that deserve our sympathy.

Fortunately, many powerful counterarguments stand at the ready. The main one is the most basic: *They're trying to change the subject! This is about women's experience, not men's.* Throughout history, and right up to the present, women have been victimized by men's violence. The vast majority of them never received any sort of justice. Most suffered their fates in silence with little recourse, due to the constraints placed on them as women in deeply misogynous, male-dominated societies that often brutally punished women who fought back or spoke out. And now finally — due to modern feminism and the incredible advances in communications technology made possible by the digital revolution — women have a voice, a platform and a way to speak and be heard about their experiences. How utterly narcissistic, petty and pathetic that these small-minded men want to take that away and make it about themselves!

Here are two more possible responses to whataboutism when you come across it:

1) Okay, you want to talk about boys and men? Let's focus for a moment on all the boys and men that have been victimized by other men's violence against the girls and women close to them. Men that harass, assault and mistreat women also do great harm to everyone that cares about them, which includes their fathers, sons, brothers, husbands, boyfriends, friends, colleagues and co-workers. I know many men whose lives have been shattered by another man's violence. Fathers whose daughters were murdered by boyfriends or husbands. Sons

whose mothers were killed by partners or exes. I know many more men whose female partners are rape survivors. The number of these men expands exponentially when you include all the men with women close to them who have been sexually abused as children or teens, groped in public, sexually harassed on the streets or in the workplace, or experienced violence and/or degrading treatment from men in countless other situations. Many of these men struggle to find ways to cope with the difficult and complex mixture of sadness, rage, guilt and relational challenges they experience as part of the ongoing legacy of this trauma. We all know such men. What about them? Some of us are such men. What about us?

2) Whataboutism posits a false choice. There is no need to choose between care and compassion for women or men. Both are victims of abuse and violence. We can and must care about all victims and survivors. Of course this includes the men and boys who are victims of violence. In fact, when it comes to crimes like murder, attempted murder, assault and aggravated assault, they are its primary victims. But it's crucial to note that the vast majority of men and boys who are victims of physical and sexual violence are *the victims of other men's violence*! Take the sexual abuse of boys, which tragically has been occurring for thousands of years but has only come to serious public attention over the

past couple of decades. The Catholic priest sexual abuse scandal is perhaps the most dramatic example of this, along with similar scandals in countless other religious denominations, sports clubs, media organizations and the like. What all these scandals have in common – beyond the violation of the trust of vulnerable children and young people by adults in positions of authority – is that the perpetrators are almost always men. The reason why is not hard to fathom: the same psychic mindset and belief system about 'manhood' that produces men who abuse women also produces men who abuse other men. To the extent that we can succeed in breaking some of the deep cultural links between masculinity, entitlement, power and control, we will effect a huge decrease in men's violence against women. And we'll also prevent a tremendous amount of physical and sexual abuse that men and boys inflict on each other.

It's About Individuals, Not Groups

One of the most common objections people raise to the premise of this book is that gender violence is not really a gender issue at all. It's certainly not a uniquely male problem; anyone can do it, and anyone can experience it. Unfortunately, people in many contemporary Western societies have a tendency to see social problems as the result of individual failures. This is perhaps even more pronounced in the United States, with its deeply rooted ethos of rugged individualism. The major exception to this in majority-white countries occurs when men of colour or immigrants are the perpetrators. In those cases, you're more likely to hear group-level explanations for misogynous abuse by men: *That's how they treat women in their culture.* White men's transgressions are more likely to be attributed to personal struggles and shortcomings, e.g. *he had an abusive childhood, he has alcohol and drug problems, he lost his job, he has mental health issues.* The neuroscientist, primatologist and bestselling author Robert Sapolsky puts it this way: 'We forgive Us more readily than Them . . . we screw up because of special circumstances; They screw up because that's how They are.'

One of the many reasons for a fixation on individual experiences of gender violence perpetration and victimization is that the violence becomes more legible when it involves real people, rather than when it's lodged in impersonal statistics or abstract calls for 'systemic' change. Moreover, sociological analysis – which furnishes invaluable insights into the underlying causes of men's violence against women – can sometimes sound academic and dry. If you want to reduce the incidence of domestic abuse, it's important to know that, historically, a key contributing factor has been a structural one: women's economic dependence on men, which for a variety of reasons has made them vulnerable to this abuse. But that's not nearly as compelling as personality-driven narratives about cruel, manipulative men and the types of women they seek out.

On the issue of domestic abuse specifically, many

members of the general public seem to have swallowed whole the propaganda from so-called men's rights organizations that women are just as likely as men to be abusers! This false equivalence fallacy is based on a highly misleading statistic, drawn from controversial early family violence research, which shows that in heterosexual relationships women hit men as often as men hit women. But this finding doesn't account for distinctions between offensive and defensive violence, size differentials between abuser and victim, whether the violence results in injury – and, crucially, whether it's a random episode or part of a pattern of coercive control. The counterintuitive (and false) argument that women and men are equally culpable goes up in smoke when these and other factors are taken into account. For example, men commit domestic assaults that result in injury three times as often as women.

For the armchair-warrior men's rights activists (MRAs) of the online manosphere, the mere suggestion that men have a role to play in ending violence against women invites a torrent of vitriol and ridicule. In the comments section of my TEDx Talk on this subject, I am regularly derided as a 'cuck', 'mangina' and 'white knight', merely for arguing that men need to do more about the global tragedy of sexual assault and domestic abuse. Why does this so easily push their buttons? The writer and *Remaking Manhood* podcaster Mark Greene has a fascinating take. 'Being told we are collectively responsible for sustaining patriarchy threatens to make us admit to ourselves that we have been bullied all our lives by the same patriarchal men who attack women.' Some of us respond angrily, he writes, 'because we must find a way to live with our own responsibility for surrendering our moral agency to bullies long ago and living with the shame that created. We know the bullies are still watching us. We're frozen/defensive in our silence.'

But if one can look past the incendiary rhetoric, it's useful to hear the arguments of MRAs, because extremists in social movements often articulate more bluntly – and with fewer filters – what many people closer to the centre might be thinking but are unwilling to say out loud. MRAs take the classic anti-feminist position that discussions about gender violence should be depoliticized. That what 'social justice warriors' want to characterize as manifestations of male dominance and misogyny are no such thing; they are really about *individual* shortcomings or pathologies. Everyone's behaviour should be assessed on the basis of their own unique personality or situation, not shoehorned into some larger pattern that furthers an ideological agenda. This is a remarkably similar line of reasoning to the one deployed by conservative whites who deny the existence of white supremacy or white privilege: those were features of the past; we're beyond all of that now. Today, most racial problems are caused by damaged or dysfunctional people, just as men who commit rape and domestic abuse are most likely troubled or deeply flawed. Real solutions reside within individuals and families, not in large-scale social or political change.

The Canadian psychologist, author and self-help guru Jordan Peterson uses his enormous platform and social media presence to offer the pretence of gravitas to right-wing anti-feminist ideas. He asserts repeatedly that the source of many social problems – and their solutions – lies in the 'sovereign individual', and that group-based claims about racial and gender inequality are largely propaganda from 'cultural Marxists'. He dismisses the feminist argument that gender inequality is one of the primary drivers of men's violence against women, and even goes so far as to deny that women face more gender-based discrimination than men. 'I . . . don't buy the argument that throughout history, men have, what would you say, singularly oppressed women?' he once said. 'I think that's absolute bloody nonsense.'

In his YouTube lectures, books and podcast interviews, Peterson tells the millions of men who revere him that concepts like 'rape culture' are insidious products of 'identity politics' movements that must be contested and defeated. He regularly makes provocative statements about sex and violence that use ideas from evolutionary psychology to reinforce conservative ideas about gender and power. He once suggested to an interviewer that women who wear make-up in the workplace essentially invite sexual attention, and are therefore being hypocritical if they object to sexual harassment. On another occasion he speculated aloud about the costs women pay for progress toward sexual freedom. He professed sympathy for the idea that the rape of a woman was no longer viewed as a property crime against the man who essentially 'owned' her. Nonetheless, he expressed concern that this major step toward women's sexual freedom made young women more vulnerable to the predations of potential rapists, because it removed one of the primary motives for her male protectors to come to her defence.

What Holds Us Back?

If so many men consider themselves 'good guys' who are not part of the problem, why do so few of them make their voices heard? Women are tired, frustrated and angry that men – even those who say they care deeply about women, and support feminist goals – are often nowhere to be found when it comes to speaking out about men's violence against women. The playwright, author and activist V (formerly Eve Ensler) expresses this in a poem called 'Over It':

I am over the passivity of good men. *Where the hell are you?*
  You live with us, make love with us, father us, befriend
  us, brother us, get nurtured and mothered and eternally
  supported by us, so why aren't you standing with us? Why
  aren't you driven to the point of madness and action by
  the rape and humiliation of us?

I won't make excuses for the passivity of good men, because there are no good excuses. I've been urging men to get off the sidelines for decades, and I have some ideas about why it's such an uphill fight:

1. Fear of other men

There is constant pressure on boys and men to conform to 'Man Box' culture – or face the consequences. One of the major fears men have dates back to our days on the playground and lingers in our psyches – the fear that we won't 'measure up' to some artificial standard of manliness, that others will find out, and that we'll be humiliated or subjected to violence from our fellow men. This fear is impossible to quantify, but it's also impossible to overstate how powerful it remains in keeping men silent about men's mistreatment of women.

The reality is that men – especially young men – who take an active stand against men's violence against women are often subject to mockery, deep scepticism and worse. It's okay if you treat women with respect, and even support their aspirations for equal treatment. But the moment you dare to question men's complicity in perpetuating a culture of misogyny, you become suspect. What sort of a cuck beta would utter that nonsense? Guys like this must have ulterior motives, because *what kind of man really cares about this subject?*

Influential men like Jordan Peterson, the podcaster Joe Rogan and Andrew Tate regularly dismiss anti-sexist men as insincere, virtue-signalling eunuchs. Maybe it's never occurred to them that we might simply be men who are repulsed by the ignorant and abusive misogyny we see all around us, and instead believe that women deserve better, and men are capable of so much more. But give them credit. Name-calling works. Many men would rather go along with the toxic status quo than face ridicule and a loss of standing as 'one of the guys' for denouncing other men's sexist beliefs and behaviours. Fortunately, if you're a man who's concerned about the issues raised in this book, you can take another path. You can fight through your doubts and anxieties about whether or not other guys will approve, and do the right thing anyway. Not incidentally, that's what leaders do, which is something we'll discuss in greater detail in chapters 6 and 7.

2. Fear of saying or doing the wrong thing

Some men are concerned that their mates will be annoyed and judge them if they take a strong anti-sexist stand, but others worry about what women will think if they say or do the wrong thing. Let's face it, men with good intentions sometimes make statements that land the wrong way with friends or colleagues, even when they're trying to be helpful. The gender debate has become so charged that some men fear one wrong step or ill-considered comment could result in hurt feelings, damaged relationships with friends or co-workers – or, in extreme cases, being 'cancelled'. So they'd rather play it safe and refrain from commenting altogether.

The therapist and bestselling author Terry Real – whose 1997 book *I Don't Want to Talk About It* was one of the first major books about men's depression, and who has worked with men as individuals and in couples over many decades – says: 'The old rules are eroding beneath our feet, and men are big-hearted, well-meaning and bewildered. We don't know what people want of us.' This confusion can lead to men opting out completely. They frequently choose to self-censor rather than risk causing offence.

In 2023 the Washington, DC-based NGO Equimundo issued the *State of American Men* report, which found that 71 per cent of men surveyed said that speaking their mind could destroy their reputation – a finding that held true for men in their late teens to early twenties and also for middle-aged men. The authors of the report described it as a sign of progress that so many men were aware that they should pause before they speak and reflect on how their words might land: 'Being held accountable for harmful, sexist, homophobic, transphobic, and racist language is a sign of genuine progress toward making shared spaces safe for all individuals.' But they also warned that the defensiveness many men feel has been weaponized by the online manosphere and the anti-feminist populist right, pushing these men away from struggles for gender justice. 'We know how to *call men out* for harm committed, but need to do a better job of *calling men in* to conversations about what is required for men to be empathic, connected, and equitable coworkers.'

3. Who am I to criticize others?

I'm not perfect myself. Who am I to lecture others? Wouldn't that make me a shameless hypocrite? This is a classic example of the old dictum that the perfect is the enemy of the good. If the standard we're setting for men to speak out about rape and sexual violence is that they 'don't have a sexist bone in their body', it's game over, because we'll never be able to find a single man who hits that mark, much less build a social movement.

It's not necessary for men to be free of any sexist taint in order for them to be effectively anti-sexist. It is necessary for them to avoid the trap of self-righteousness – the idea that they're evolved and other men are knuckle-draggers. I try to make a point of saying in my talks and trainings that I'm a long way from having it all figured out. The good news is that men don't need to be paragons of virtue in order to move the ball forward. We are all a work in progress. Mostly we need to be open to introspection, and willing to take some risks to break our complicit silence.

4. Pretzel logic

Sometimes men who are fully conscious of the dimensions of the global crisis of men's violence against women nonetheless remain silent or less than fully engaged because they've tied themselves up in knots of confusion and indecision surrounding matters of privilege and responsibility. In the 1990s, I was at a meeting in Boston of anti-sexist men's groups. We were planning a public action in which men would speak out about gender violence. One of the men kept objecting to various suggestions that others made about the goals of the event, the target audience, what sort of outreach we should make to media, etc. He was clearly uncomfortable with men making these sorts of decisions, or even the very idea of organizing an event about violence against women that would call attention to men. Weren't we, as men, supposed to be creating space for women's voices? If we raised our voices too loudly, wouldn't we just be reinforcing the traditional patriarchal dynamic, in which men's voices count more than women's?

After a few exchanges like this, one of the other men lost patience with the guy. 'If you have all these qualms,' he asked sharply, 'why are you even in a men's group?' Good question! It turns out he was, in fact, more comfortable with men working quietly in the background for feminist women's organizations, doing important but menial tasks like stuffing envelopes and lugging bags of mail to the post office. He hadn't got the memo that anti-sexist men need to take initiative on their own, and not always put the burden on women to tell them what they can and should do in the struggle for gender justice.

But he's not alone. To this day, many men are unsure of whether or not they have an active role to play. They have heard women say loud and clear that it's time for men to sit down, be quiet and really *listen* to women's voices – especially what they have to say about their experiences of sexism and men's violence. Fair enough. If they listened a little closer, they would also hear a chorus of women voices – dating back to the 1970s – that tell supportive men and would-be allies that they need to get out there and educate, organize and politicize other men.

5. The false choice fallacy

Should we attend to men's wounds first, and when they get healthier, then get to work on sexist violence? Or is confronting men's violence against women the front line of the struggle that cannot be deferred? This is a false choice. We can – and must – do both at the same time.

In recent years, we have become more aware of and open about the interior lives of men. Conversations in the media have spotlighted the issues of men's mental health, in schools and in the workplace; drug, alcohol, sex and gaming addictions; chronic loneliness; and high rates of suicide. Of course, these problems boys and men face are exacerbated for boys and men of colour, who are forced to deal with the additional burden of coping with covert and overt racism. All this increased attention to the struggles of men is welcome, but it's important to note that feminist women and pro-feminist men have been thinking, writing and advocating for the social and emotional needs of boys and young men since the 1970s. In my own work, for example, I have always drawn connections between narrow and constrained definitions of 'manhood' and the violence that men both experience and commit. My first educational documentary was called *Tough Guise: Violence, Media, and the Crisis in Masculinity* (1999), and it addressed directly how boys are forced to conform to unhealthy and often self-destructive masculinity norms, and the ways in which these are reinforced by powerful narratives in entertainment and media culture.

It should be well beyond debate at this point that untold numbers of boys and men across the world are harmed by restrictive masculinity norms. This is especially true of men who do not identify as traditionally masculine and heteronormative – and are therefore more vulnerable to harassment and violence from other men and male-dominant systems. But men's violence against women is a widespread human rights violation that needs to be addressed in its own right – whether or not men suffer too.

Fortunately, all of this is connected. The violence and trauma so many boys experience in childhood and adolescence – in their families and beyond – is one of the root causes of their subsequent violence toward women, other men and themselves. In theory, the way out is simple. The more we raise boys in healthy, loving, non-violent families and communities, the less likely they will be to dominate, control and hurt women or anyone else.

How You Can Make a Difference

Contemporary debates about the underlying causes of gender-based violence, and the appropriate role for men in fighting against it, go back more than fifty years. Of course, there have been stunning technological developments that have created new opportunities and dilemmas. But when it comes to the core question of men's individual versus collective responsibilities on this topic, there's nothing new under the sun. Many arguments against the central premise of this book are old, entirely predictable and easy to counter. I have provided you with some basic lines of rebuttal. I recommend that if you have occasion to debate the topics in this book, either with friends or in more public settings, you bring up some of those contrary arguments pre-emptively whenever possible. That way you can demonstrate that you've carefully considered the critics' point of view, and have still come down on the side of believing that violence against women is a men's issue.

5. Language Matters

'Not everything that is faced can be changed, but
nothing can be changed until it is faced.'
– James Baldwin

Is it anti-male to tell the truth? Do facts discriminate against men? If not, then why do so many people find it hard to use clear, accountable language when they talk about gender-based violence? It might seem obvious, but the first and perhaps the most straightforward step we can take to alter perceptions on this issue is to examine and change the language we use to think, speak and write about it. I know that something meaningful shifted in my consciousness when I first encountered critiques of the many ways in which sexist language shapes and distorts our thinking. I want this chapter to do that for you as well: specifically, to help you better analyse the language we use to talk about gender violence, along with providing some concrete suggestions about how to improve the clarity and effectiveness of the way you think and communicate on this critical topic.

I had one of those rare 'light bulb' moments when I first encountered the ideas of the late American feminist linguist Julia Penelope in the early 1990s. I came across something she had written about passive language and its role in perpetuating men's violence against women, and it forever changed the way I thought and wrote about the subject. I had been searching for creative new strategies to engage men on this issue. But when I started to pay close attention to what people said – or didn't say – in discussions about gender-based violence, I noticed that men were barely even mentioned.

Penelope explained that this doesn't happen by accident, but is literally built into the structures of the language we use to think and talk about these matters. The misdeeds of the powerful are very often hidden – sometimes in plain sight. One of the chief ways this works in discussions about gender violence is through passive language (e.g. 'She was the victim of sexual harassment' versus 'He sexually harassed her'). The shift from active to passive voice takes the focus off abusers and puts it onto victims. It's a subtle but powerful type of victim-blaming that helps men evade accountability – at the level of sentence structure – even as it reinforces the sexist belief that women are ultimately responsible for men's behaviour.

Once you see this in the language it's impossible to unsee. Most conversations about 'violence against women' are suffused with passive language. Take, for example, the ways in which people inquire about the incidence of sexual assault. They might ask 'How many women were raped on university campuses in the UK last year?' or 'How many girls in this school district have been sexually harassed?' By contrast, it's highly unusual to hear someone say 'How many men raped women at university?' or 'How many boys harassed girls?' This matters because we're less likely to zero in on boys and men as a key source of the *solution* if we can't even bring ourselves to identify them as a key source of the *problem*.

Let's look at teen pregnancy. People will say 'How many teenage girls *got pregnant*?' – but when was the last time you heard someone ask: 'How many men and boys impregnated teenage girls?' Passive language also impedes clarity when it comes to anti-trans bigotry and violence. This is exemplified by common use of the passive phrase 'violence against transgender women of colour'. We know they experience awful discrimination and violence. But who's committing it, and why? How can we prevent it from happening if we can't even mention who's responsible for it? The ubiquitous phrase 'violence against women' is itself part of the problem. It suggests that something terrible is happening to women, but no one is actually making it happen.

As I mentioned at the start of chapter 1, when you insert what linguists call the 'active agent' – *men* – a new phrase emerges: 'men's violence against women'. It doesn't roll off the tongue as easily, but it's more accurate – and honest. Women do assault other women – mother-to-daughter child abuse and intimate partner violence in lesbian relationships are two cases in point. But men commit the vast majority of violence against women in the world. That's a simple statement of fact. Again, is it anti-male to say that? Is it anti-male to tell the truth?

One of the central ideas of this book is that we need to think differently about the very old problem of men's violence against women. If language is the means by which we construct and analyse what we call 'reality', then any serious effort to change reality begins with efforts to examine and change the way we think, speak and write about it. This work is already well under way in the area of gender-based violence. Over the last twenty years, advocacy groups have campaigned successfully for language guidelines that are used by journalists who report on and write about sexual and domestic abuse. Journalists should now refer to adults having sex with children as 'rape' instead of 'sex with a child', and they should refrain from using language that talks about sexual violence in a voyeuristic way, such as describing sexual crimes against children in graphic detail. Anyone who wants information about how to overhaul language usage in this area should see the notes section for links to this literature.

But shifting popular consciousness is no easy task — especially because victim-blaming is embedded in normative language. In discussions about gender violence, the focus often defaults to what the woman did or didn't do – as if the man is not an active participant in the events described – or even present! If she was sexually assaulted, it was probably at least in part because she sent the wrong signals. If she was physically or verbally abused, it must have been something she did or said. Maybe she provoked him. Maybe she didn't understand him well enough. Maybe she wasn't meeting his needs. But *his* violence was somehow caused by *her*. If only *she* had done better, all of this could have been avoided. But what about him? His responsibility remains hidden in the very language we use to talk about this.

People who run court-mandated groups for men who abuse – the first of which was started more than forty years ago – know all too well that men who abuse their partners are often the masters of denial, minimization and passive language; anything to avoid taking responsibility for their own behaviour. *There was a fight last night.* Or: *She went and got herself beat up.* The group facilitators consider it a breakthrough when the men start using 'I' statements that acknowledge their behaviour as the source of harm. But in or out of offenders' groups, the prevalence of this sort of linguistic evasion of accountability is precisely why we need a reframe. It's amazing how different the world looks when you use active voice, and it's equally amazing how new pathways for progress emerge.

The Australian journalist Jess Hill opens her book about domestic abuse, *See What You Made Me Do*, with an anecdote about a conversation she had with women who were working for a family violence helpline. After noting that, on average, women go back to their abuser seven times before they finally leave, she said to them, 'You must get so frustrated when you think a woman is ready to leave and then she decides to go back.' 'No,' one phone counsellor pointedly replied. 'I'm frustrated that even though he promised to stop, he chose to abuse her again.'

Language about gender violence that explicitly focuses on men, or shines the critical spotlight on their behaviour, is still relatively rare and noteworthy. My intent here is very specific: to open your eyes to the many ways in which the language commonly used to talk about men's violence against women keeps our focus off those most responsible for committing it, as well as the culture that produces them.

It's important to acknowledge that many women themselves hesitate to use active, direct and gender-specific language to talk about men's violence, because they are rightly and realistically concerned about potential blowback and hostility from offended or angry men – in both their personal and professional lives, as well as on social media and other online spaces. Some women can't say these things – or utter certain truths – because it's physically unsafe for them to do so. That's yet another reason why men need to speak up – to take some of this pressure off women. Let's be clear. This is not about blaming and shaming men; it's about honesty. It's about naming the problem accurately so we can have a thoughtful discussion about its causes and solutions. We're not going to solve a problem we can't even bring ourselves to name.

I want to help change that, and show what's wrong with how we talk about men's role in gender violence, by focusing on five different areas of language usage: passive voice, omission, gender-neutral language, media (mis)coverage of misogyny, and the problematic phrase 'toxic masculinity'.

Passive Voice

Let's take a closer look at how using the passive voice works so effectively to take the spotlight off of men, or even to absolve them of responsibility. I created the exercise below based on the work of Julia Penelope. Consider these statements as they appear in turn:

John beat Mary.
Mary was beaten by John.

Mary was beaten.
Mary was abused.
Mary is an abused woman.

The sequence begins with the statement that 'John beat Mary', a perfectly formed English sentence made up of subject-verb-object. John did something wrong – he beat Mary. But the meaning changes when you use passive language. One sentence down, it's '*Mary* was beaten by John'. The focus turns to what happened to Mary, and John is relegated to the end of the sentence. The third sentence is 'Mary was beaten', and John is now gone. Mary is our sole focus. We often replace the word 'beaten' with 'abused', as in the next sentence – 'Mary was abused'. The final sentence, 'Mary is an abused woman', suggests that Mary's very identity – *an abused woman* – is defined by what John did to her. But John has disappeared completely; he has successfully evaded accountability for his actions.

In other words, the passive voice is not just bad writing. It also has political implications, i.e. it shifts responsibility for abuse and violence from the abuser (John) to the abused (Mary). We of course need to make sure that Mary is safe and gets whatever services and treatment she needs. But that won't solve the underlying problem. That has to do with John and why he beat Mary, and what that says not only about him as an individual, or his family of origin, but also about the culture that produced him.

According to the World Health Organization, worldwide almost one-third of women aged 15–49 who have been in a relationship have experienced some form of physical or sexual violence from their 'intimate partner'.

The vast number of these are men. Are they all 'bad apples'? Or does this astounding and shameful number tell us something about societal norms and the retrograde beliefs about masculinity, respect, entitlement and power that are still disturbingly present – and even promoted – in the world today? Does it tell us something about how men have and have not adjusted to women's economic gains and growing independence from traditional patri-archal controls? How are we going to ask and answer these sorts of questions if we can't even use direct and honest language?

Omission

Another problem to recognize is how often men are omit-ted from official statements or news stories covering instances of violence against women. Take this statement made by United Nations Secretary-General António Guterres in 2020. 'Violence against women and girls is a pervasive global human rights challenge, rooted in unequal gender power relations, structural inequality and discrim-ination.' So far, so good. Yet throughout the statement, he refers repeatedly to 'violence against women and girls' and 'gender-based violence', says that 'all forms of violence against them are rising' due to COVID-19, and that 'vio-lence against women and girls is a horrible and widespread affront to their human rights, and a blight on all our soci-eties'. The statement mentions men and boys only once.

Josep Borrell Fontelles, High Representative of the European Union for Foreign Affairs and Security Policy, took the globally recognized occasion of the 16 Days of Activism Against Gender-Based Violence 2022 to announce a number of important initiatives that included a new EU-wide helpline for victims, and special attention to the needs of victims and survivors in conflict areas. 'It is unacceptable in the 21st century', said his statement, 'that women and girls continue to be abused, harassed, raped, mutilated or forced into marriage.' But he didn't say who was abusing, harassing, raping and mutilating them, or forcing them into marriage. Or offer any ideas about what he and his wealthy and powerful organization could do about *that* part of the equation.

Pope Francis met with an Italian law enforcement group on 25 November 2022, the International Day for the Elimination of Violence Against Women that serves as the kick-off for the 16 Days. In statements he made that day, the Pope emphasized the need for prevention – which, he noted, 'is always crucial when trying to eliminate a social scourge which is also linked to cultural attitudes, mentalities and deep-rooted prejudices'. But even in the reported comments about prevention, he didn't say anything specifically about men.

Why not? In what conceivable way can prevention be successful without directly engaging and mobilizing men? A cynic might reasonably argue that it is not realistic to expect leaders of deeply patriarchal organizations like the Catholic Church to highlight men's abuses of power, especially when the Church has attracted a torrent of criticism from activists for more than twenty years over its abysmal handling of sexual abuse cases by Catholic clergymen. Fair enough. But if accountability means anything, we need to hold powerful men accountable for not using the giant platforms they have to address the crisis of men's violence against women more forthrightly and assertively. And that means urging them to turn their attention to the ways in which men – including other powerful men – can create space for enhanced dialogues about the roles and responsibilities of men. Imagine the progress we could make if influential men in positions like the head of the UN, heads of state, or the Pope regularly made statements about men's violence against women that included language that looked like the following:

> As a man I want to acknowledge in unequivocal terms that violence against women is a men's issue – for men, young men and boys from every ethnic, racial and religious group all over the world. This scourge will not be eliminated until each and every one of us decides to do our part to make this happen. This includes boys and young men who need to make it clear to their friends and peers that misogyny and all forms of abuse are not okay, and you will lose status amongst your peers if you treat girls and women with disrespect in any way – verbally, physically or sexually. But I especially want to address my fellow adult men. We need to do whatever we can within our spheres of influence to challenge the misogynous attitudes and beliefs that underlie sexual assault, domestic abuse, and too many other crimes and abuses that cause multitudes of women and girls – and those who love them – so much unnecessary pain and suffering. This does not mean we need to ignore the needs of men and

boys – far from it. Or the needs of anyone outside of traditional binary identities. We are all interdependent, and our lives and fates are intertwined. We need to forge new ways to be men in an evolving world, and this includes moving past the old, tired and discredited idea that might makes right, or that men's violence against women can be justified and defended by appeals to tradition, or any other ethical, religious or natural law rationalization. The status quo is unacceptable. We can and must do better. And we need to work alongside women as their partners, allies and collaborators to make this happen.

Gender-Neutral Language

Echoing a long-standing feminist precept, I wrote in my first book, *The Macho Paradox,* that we cannot achieve dramatic reductions in men's violence against women until we can at least *name* the problem accurately. At present, few people view this violence the way I've described it in these pages: as a *men's* problem or a *men's* issue. One consequence of this failure is that little discussion occurs in media – or anywhere else – about why so many men and boys rape, batter, sexually abuse and sexually harass women and girls. Mainstream commentary about gender violence – and other forms of interpersonal violence – is remarkably degendered. We use gender-neutral language to talk about a problem that is largely gender-specific. It's almost as if journalists, educators and even activists make a conscious effort not to bring up the fact that men and boys commit the vast majority of violence against women and other men. Instead, we hear regular reports about the 'people' who commit these crimes. On a related note, the US has experienced hundreds of school shootings since what I refer to as the era of school shootings was inaugurated in 1998; 99 per cent of those shootings were committed by boys or young men. But to this day, we wring our hands about yet another tragic incident of 'kids killing kids'.

In one sense it is easy to see why mainstream language about gender violence is typically gender-neutral. If we talked about it as a *men's* problem, if we asked 'Why do *men* commit these awful crimes?' the language itself would shift the spotlight to men, and this would make a lot of people – men, women and others – uncomfortable. It would reinvigorate a long-dormant conversation that began in the 1970s, and point us toward a series of probing and unsettling questions: why do so many men assault women? What is the process by which millions of loving little boys grow up and turn into controlling, abusive men? What role do narrow and restrictive ideas about masculinity play in it? How are those ideas passed down within families, but also by the culture itself? Why do so many men sexually harass women and girls? Why do so many grown men sexually abuse children – girls and boys? Did #MeToo have a lasting impact on men's behaviour, or has the backlash against it reversed any progress that was made? And why is it still the case that relatively few men with a public platform have spoken out forcefully about men's violence against women?

It has been in vogue in recent years to seek explanations for human behaviour not in social structures but in biology or evolutionary psychology. But how do those disciplines account for the wide variation across different cultures in rates of rape, domestic violence and other controlling and abusive behaviours? Genetics doesn't vary across cultures, but social structures and belief systems about gender and power certainly do. So, if the problem is not on the 'nature' but rather on the 'nurture' side of the equation, what are we doing wrong? How can we help shape the socialization of boys to counteract whatever forces in our culture help to produce so many abusive men? For now, the absence of clear, direct language about men's perpetration practically guarantees that we barely ask – much less answer – these critical questions.

Media (Mis)Coverage of Misogyny

Media commentary about gender violence often obscures as much as it reveals about underlying gender norms and how they contribute to the problem. A powerful illustration of this can be found in media coverage of an incident that happened during a high school ice hockey game in a suburb of Pittsburgh, Pennsylvania, in early November 2021.

One of the teams featured a young woman playing in goal who was the only female player on either team. As the teams took to the ice, a cheering section of young (white) men began to taunt the girl with a chant, yelling 'she's a whore' and 'suck my dick'. The story became a sensation when it became clear that none of the adults present – either coaches or parents who were in attendance – intervened to stop the abusive chants. The incident generated much local news coverage, in print and on TV, with most reporters and commentators condemning the behaviour of the fans and bemoaning the fact that, during the offensive tirade, few spoke out to defend the young woman.

Alas, much of that coverage, and the commentaries it generated, failed to address squarely – or even name – the normalization of misogyny at the heart of this disturbing incident. A case in point was an opinion piece by Paul Zeise, a columnist for the *Pittsburgh Post-Gazette*. Zeise rightly expressed outrage at the behaviour of the crowd. He was particularly scornful of the parents, officials and other adults present who did nothing to stop the verbal abuse. But not once in his article did he mention that 1) the chanters were all young men and 2) the chants were not just offensive in a general sense, but were deeply misogynous.

Zeise explicitly mentioned gender in the article, but only when he was referring to the 'female hockey goalie' or when he referenced an organization that worked with 'women who have been victims of abuse'. Whenever he was discussing the instigators of the abusive chant, he switched to gender-neutral terms. He called them 'kids', 'students' and 'young people', and expressed disdain for anyone who would dismiss their behaviour as just 'kids being kids'.

This is consistent with a widespread pattern in the way journalists describe the phenomena of domestic violence and sexual assault: the targets and victims of misogynous violence are identified as women, while the perpetrators are described in gender-neutral terms like 'spouse', 'abuser' or 'assailant'. Headlines feature sentences like 'Woman, 37, murdered by spouse' or 'Girls at primary school targeted for harassment by classmates'. It's as if the writers are either reluctant to say explicitly that it's men or young men who are doing these things, or they are so immersed in writing from an androcentric point of view that it never even occurs to them to gender the perpetrators. Why bother when it's obvious that it's men? Why risk redundancy by saying it out loud? The trouble is that when the gender of the perpetrators is not written down or overtly mentioned, subsequent discussions about the motives that underlie their actions omit the crucial gender subtext. Instead, one hears – as in the incident in the hockey arena – that the 'students' were 'ignorant' and in need of adult guidance about the possible harmful effects of their cruel comments.

To be sure, the columnist condemned the actions of the young men – even if he didn't name them as such – and said they needed to understand why the attitudes they had 'toward women' could escalate 'from abusive language to abusive actions if they go unchecked'. But he did not use the word 'sexism', or 'misogyny', which might have helped put the event into a sociocultural and political perspective. This wasn't simply a group of immature high school students taunting a player on an opposing team. This was a group of young men mocking, ridiculing and sexualizing a young woman athlete who had the temerity to impinge on a male space by integrating into the hockey team. This was about a historically privileged group (men) asserting its prerogatives by punishing a member of an outside group (women) who was invading home territory.

It is not enough to see sexist or racist behaviour as merely 'intolerance' – or, in the case of sexism, 'laddish' callousness and cruelty. This type of abusive behaviour also plays a powerful role in maintaining the existing social order. Along these lines, the philosopher Kate Manne, in her book *Down Girl*, argues that misogyny is not merely the hatred of women. Instead, she calls it the 'law enforcement branch' of a patriarchal order that serves to police and enforce men's dominant social position. The idea is that when women refuse to conform to dictates about living in a 'man's world', or seek to challenge men's power, they are punished for it – frequently by being sexualized or instructed about their sexual subservience to men. The hockey incident is a textbook example of the sort of sexual harassment that frequently occurs in formerly all-male workplaces – a deliberate attempt by men to create a hostile environment in a bid to make women feel uncomfortable, and eventually force them out. Whether or not the adolescent boys screaming at the female goalie were conscious of the ways in which they were playing the role of guardians of an old order in a larger sociohistorical struggle, that's exactly what they were doing.

If the taunting in the Pennsylvania hockey arena was in fact a teachable moment, as Paul Zeise surely believed, all of these gendered dynamics should have been part of the lessons learned. But however genuine his outrage and disappointment, his critique of that sad incident was hampered – like so many other accounts of so many other incidents – by his failure to name the gender of the perpetrators, the misogyny that fuelled their actions, and the persistent gender inequality that is the necessary precondition for all this to have occurred in the first place.

Toxic Masculinity

I try to avoid using it, but 'toxic masculinity' is one of the signature phrases of this cultural moment. It's unusual to read a story about sexual harassment or assault these days and not encounter the term. It's used to describe a set of harmful behaviours that include not only misogyny, but also participation in or glorification of violence – including men's violence against other men, rigid adherence to heteronormative understandings of gender, hyper-competitiveness, poor self-care, and other sorts of reckless and risk-taking behaviours. To the extent that it gets people to use the word 'masculinity' in analyses of men's abusive and violent behaviour, the term 'toxic masculinity' plays a constructive role, because gender norms are so integral to the commission of most forms of violence, and thus should always be part of the conversation.

But overall I don't think it's a helpful phrase. What's wrong with it? For one thing it causes a lot of confusion. Many men – especially on the political right – think it's the ultimate expression of anti-male sentiment: they think (incorrectly) that it means masculinity itself is toxic, and that men as a whole are irredeemable. But I also don't like the term because the poison metaphor emphasizes biology, not ideology, and thus represents yet another example of what sociologists refer to as the 'biologization of everything'. A toxin is a poison, so when you say something is toxic, you're saying an organic entity has been poisoned. But 'masculinity' is not some pristine body that's vulnerable to invasion. It is a set of human characteristics that a given society assigns to people who are born with XY chromosomes (typically juxtaposed against those born with XX chromosomes, who are assigned characteristics deemed to be markers of 'femininity'), as well as a set of relations and behaviours that reinforce, reproduce and sometimes redefine identities. Those gendered characteristics are assigned on the basis of traditions including religious belief, economic necessity, and other factors by which a society socializes and organizes people to function within institutions like the family, the economy, government, the military, etc. Different societies have different ideas about how to do that, which is why it is more accurate to understand masculinity (as opposed to maleness) as an ideology or belief system than as a biological entity that can be polluted.

'Toxic masculinity' is also misleading because it emphasizes the problem in individual terms – as in, 'his toxic masculinity'. But is violent behaviour the product of individual pathology, or is it a social problem? One might say it's both – that individuals possess unique characteristics, but they're also profoundly influenced by social scripts that include gender norms. It is notable, however, that gendered behaviour – especially around the use of violence – is often explained as a problem of 'sick' individuals in a way that other behaviour is not. Why are terms like 'toxic whiteness' and 'toxic heterosexuality' relatively rare, while 'toxic masculinity' has become a ubiquitous phrase?

Many people assume incorrectly that 'toxic masculinity' is a phrase invented by feminists as yet another way to bash men. In fact, the term was introduced sometime in the late 1980s by a man named Shepherd Bliss, who was well known then as a leading voice in the 'mythopoetic' men's movement. This movement, most prominently identified with the late poet and *Iron John* author Robert Bly, was in part a reaction to Second Wave feminism and the challenge it posed to traditional ideas about men's nature and their socially assigned roles. The term was meant to refer to negative expressions of aggression and other distorted acting-out behaviours of modern men who had been cut off from the 'deep masculine' characteristics of ancient warriors, kings and other Jungian archetypes, and denied the rites of passage and rituals that could connect them with their true selves. In its usage by the mythopoetics, 'toxic masculinity' wasn't meant as a criticism of men, but rather as a lamentation of how modernity had wounded them.

In its current usage, 'toxic masculinity' names the harm but does little to offer men a positive identity. My friend and colleague Don McPherson, a former National Football League quarterback and member of the College Football Hall of Fame, has been working with men on issues of misogyny and violence since the 1990s. He emphasizes the need to give boys and young men the language and tools to transcend the limitations of narrow and often 'toxic' ideas about manhood. 'We need to instill the belief that our boys are capable of and worthy of excellence,' he says. McPherson describes realizing that, in discussions about preventing men's violence against women, not much was being offered to men other than an indictment of their silence, and the conclusion that their identity needed to be redefined or dismantled entirely. By contrast, he advocates an 'aspirational masculinity' that includes empathy, vulnerability and emotional honesty around critical issues impacting relationships, sexual behaviour and personal growth. Or as Ben Hurst, director of facilitation and training at Beyond Equality, said in his TEDx Talk: we need to 'celebrate the good parts' of being a man, but also give men spaces to unpack the problematic messages they have learned about what it means to be a man that are 'harmful and damaging to themselves and others'. Most importantly, Hurst said, 'we need to have the conversations.'

How You Can Make a Difference

I'm not a trained linguist, but I am an educator. And I know that when you help people think about *how* they think, it has ripple effects on their consciousness and often pays dividends down the road. If you, the reader, have never thought about some of the ways in which you talk about gender violence, I hope this chapter has helped you see these issues in a new light. And here's a suggestion. If you have friends who ask you about this book, share the 'John beat Mary' exercise with them. And then tell them the book is about why he did that — and what all of us can do to make sure it never happens again.

6. The Bystander Approach: How Everyone Can Make a Difference

'The worst crimes were dared by a few, willed by
more, and tolerated by all.'
– Tacitus, Roman historian, first century CE

'Once bystanders begin to take a righteous stand in
support of survivors, the power of the tyrant
begins to crumble. For this reason, repairing the
harms of tyranny first of all requires bystanders
and the larger community to recognize their own
moral responsibility and to take action in solidarity
with those who have been harmed.'
– Judith L. Herman, MD, *Truth and Repair*

If you're reading this and feeling a bit overwhelmed,
the good news is that you can help. Whether you're
with a group of friends, classmates or teammates, playing poker with the guys, or just interacting with
co-workers or colleagues, you can put some of what you
will learn in this chapter to use straight away in your daily
life. I'm going to introduce you to some of the basic
components of the bystander approach, which is one
of the leading educational strategies in gender violence

prevention education in North America and around the world. I and others have been developing bystander training – sometimes called bystander intervention – since the early 1990s, and it is currently growing in popularity in the UK. It has been implemented in most of the public high school districts in Scotland, as well as parts of Ireland, Sweden, Australia and elsewhere.

The plan is to run you through some real-life scenarios that will give you a good idea of the applied ethical decision-making process you will go through in order to make good choices about how to intervene before, during or after incidents of gender-based abuse or violence. But before you get to the specifics in the second half of this chapter, I want to give you some background about the history and rationale behind bystander training.

An Overview of Bystander Training

Throughout this book I have maintained that we need to change the social acceptability of misogyny in male culture at all levels. In order for that to happen, men must make it clear to their friends, teammates, colleagues and co-workers that misogynous behaviour – from catcalls to gang rape and everything in between – is not only wrong and sometimes illegal, it's also uncool and unwelcome for their fellow men (as well as women and non-binary people). This is a seemingly simple thing to grasp in principle, but it's been incredibly difficult to achieve in practice, because millions of men who see themselves as 'good guys' and not part of the problem nonetheless often fail to act when they could make a difference.

What are some of the main obstacles to them doing so? There has been some generational progress and a growing acceptance of diverse masculinities and gender fluidity. But the expansion of the online manosphere, the normalization of deeply misogynous porn, the enormous popularity of influencers like Andrew Tate, and above all the persistence of alarming rates of men's violence against women suggest that some features of traditional male peer cultures are alive and well. Boys and men continue to face intense pressure to be 'one of the guys' and not rock the boat – or risk facing the consequences. This pressure is impossible to quantify, but it's also impossible to overstate how powerful it remains in keeping men silent about men's mistreatment of women.

The pressure to remain silent in order to fit in affects men across the board, but it's intensified for men who are part of cohesive organizational cultures. These can be informal, such as street gangs or darts teams, or formal, such as (men's) sports teams, law enforcement agencies and military units. Men in these male-dominated subcultures share not only mutual goals, but often deep bonds of camaraderie and friendship. The downside is that individuals are expected to conform to the rules of hierarchy and not challenge group norms, or risk social penalties and in some cases social or professional suicide. These norms can encourage and reward either prosocial or antisocial behaviour. The respect for status hierarchies in most male-dominated social or professional peer cultures has obvious implications for bystander behaviour, because men who are younger, or who have less social status or power, know they risk a great deal if they call out misogynous behaviour by more senior or more popular colleagues – regardless of what it says in the team's code of conduct or workplace employee handbook.

The social dynamics in peer cultures can make it difficult for people to intervene – even when it is their job to do so. Whether it's called a boy code, a guy code or a bro code, a set of unwritten rules governs the behaviour of individuals in all-male or male-dominated groups. This is especially true of groups engaged in aggressive competition and 'us versus them' battles with other groups – this is the case in sport and politics, and is even more pronounced in military or paramilitary organizations such as the police. For example, in 2023, Baroness Louise Casey's highly critical report on the Metropolitan Police found a 'boys' club culture' of racism, misogyny and homophobia. In the case of the Met, the internal culture of the force drew even greater scrutiny and expressions of outrage from advocates for women when reports surfaced that police officials had not followed up on prior multiple allegations by women of indecent exposure by officer Wayne Couzens, who went on to rape and murder Sarah Everard.

Race, ethnicity and other factors also play a role in who feels authorized to speak up in a given situation, what they might say or do, whether someone is more or less likely to be heard, and what risks they take if they do intervene. For example, in bystander trainings in the States, I've heard Black men describe a very different thought process than that of most white men about whether they would intervene in certain circumstances. Many Black men say that in a potential sexual assault scenario at a party, they would hesitate to become the active bystander who gets involved because of their well-founded fear that if the police were called, they might arrive and make the racist assumption that the Black man was the assailant – rather than being the person trying to help.

When I created the Mentors in Violence Prevention (MVP) programme to work with male athletes in the early 1990s, the first major challenge we faced was the question of how we could break through men's defensiveness. How could we put into practice Esta Soler's adage and 'invite, not indict' them? That led us to incorporate and adapt a dynamic new framework – the bystander approach – that would bring everyone in a given peer culture – but especially men – into the conversation.

The bystander idea had already been germinating in the area of middle school bullying prevention. The rationale behind it was simple. Instead of putting the focus on the bully and the bullied, it focused on everybody else. What could they do to express solidarity and support for the person being bullied, and at the same time make it clear to the one causing harm that his/her/their behaviour wasn't okay? In other words, what were some of the ways in which the peer culture could police itself?

We applied this model to gender violence prevention, and it immediately gave us a way to speak to young men who said 'this is not my problem'. Our message became, and remains: it's good if you don't abuse women – but it's not good enough. What are you doing to interrupt and challenge the casual misogyny of men around you? What do you say when a friend makes a degrading comment about women's bodies? When a poster in an online community you belong to makes a victim-blaming comment about a sexual assault survivor? When your friend chastises and humiliates his girlfriend in front of others? If you don't do or say anything, isn't your silence a form of consent and complicity in this misogynous behaviour? Let's talk about what you could say or do – before, during and/or after the fact – that communicates your disapproval or might help to defuse a difficult situation.

The bystander approach quickly caught on. Guys liked the idea that they weren't being spoken *to* as perpetrators or potential abusers, but instead spoken *with* as people who could make a positive difference. Since then, this approach that invites men (and others) to act and be a better version of themselves – for the benefit of women, men and the community as a whole – has successfully been rolled out within MVP programmes on sports teams, but also in high schools, universities, business, the military, and countless other organizations in and outside of the education sector.

Gender Transformative Programming

Many different types of 'bystander' programmes operate today across North America, and parts of the UK, Europe, Australia and elsewhere – but they're not all alike. Various programmes interpret and operationalize bystander philosophy differently. For example, unlike some bystander intervention programmes that emphasize the development of personal skills ('self-efficacy') and downplay or discourage potentially contentious debates about gender/masculinity, the model that I teach encourages open dialogue about the specific ways in which beliefs about manhood, such as the 'guy code', dictate what men are willing – and not willing – to say and do in response to misogynous behaviour on the part of their friends and peers.

This is consistent with the 'gender transformative' approach that is practised by NGOs around the world and favoured by many of my colleagues in the movement to engage and mobilize men. Gender transformative prevention programmes that target men prioritize the discussion of gender norms and cultural ideas about men and masculinities. These norms and ideas contribute not only to men's violence against women, but also to other harmful behaviours that men, young men, and boys take up – everything from risk-taking behaviours like unprotected sex to reluctance to access routine medical care. (Note: there are gender transformative programmes that focus on girls and women too.)

At its core, bystander training should be about more than reacting in real time to dramatic incidents. That's more like nightclub bouncer training. People – especially young men – need *permission* from each other to act, and reassurance that those who do interrupt misogynous comments and intervene when it comes to abusive behaviour will be respected, not rejected, for actually 'lifting their head above the parapet'. The aim is to *en*courage each other to be better, not simply to *dis*courage them when they get it wrong.

When sexual assault prevention educators talk about bystanders – unless they're explicitly referring to incidents that happen in public spaces – they usually mean people who know each other. The dynamics of bystander behaviour – and the impediments to action – are very different in known peer cultures, in which people have pre-existing relationships with the perpetrator and/or victim, versus when they are strangers. In fact, many people confuse the bystander *effect* with the bystander *approach*, but there is a key difference.

The bystander effect is a social psychological concept that explains why people who encounter difficult or dangerous situations on the street or in other public places such as the Tube often fail to act. Many people don't want to get involved in situations of potential harassment or violence in which they don't know the parties involved, largely out of fear of putting themselves at *physical* risk. In the States this fear is heightened dramatically because there are more than 400 million guns in circulation. People know the decision to be a Good Samaritan could end up with them getting shot and killed.

The bystander effect describes the mindset of people who, as members of a crowd, might hesitate to act because they expect – and hope! – that someone else will jump in. By contrast, when bystanders know the people involved in some sort of interpersonal conflict or violence – such as members of their own family or friendship circle, or their colleagues in the workplace – their hesitancy to get involved is typically based on *social* fear, i.e. the anxiety that if they criticize another man's attitudes or behaviour toward women, it could get awkward, and might cause a rift in the friendship or have other negative repercussions. Think about men in college fraternities, on sports teams and in C-suites or blue-collar workplaces. In some cases – depending on the relative popularity of the respective parties – speaking up might result in a loss of status in the group. So when men see their friends, teammates or colleagues act in negative ways toward women, they choose the path of least resistance, which is to keep their head down, say nothing and do nothing – and hope the moment passes. The bystander approach teaches us that we all have a responsibility to not be silent, and hence complicit, when people around us perpetuate or experience harms.

A Dialogue, Not a Lecture

It is clear by now that one key to engaging people in violence prevention – especially men – is to involve rather than dictate. That is why the model I teach encourages robust dialogues organized around a range of scenarios that position young (and older) men, women and non-binary people as bystanders in situations that cover a continuum of abuses, from seemingly innocuous sexist comments to cyber-bullying and harassment, all the way to brutal gang rapes. (Note: from the beginning, MVP training has also addressed male-on-male violence, women's violence against men as well as other women, violence against LGBTQ people, etc.) These scenarios often involve socially complex dynamics that require processing. My colleagues and I favour a highly interactive, experiential workshop style for this reason.

Graham Goulden, a former Chief Inspector and key member of Police Scotland's Violence Reduction Unit, who does bystander training with law enforcement personnel, educators and others across the UK, Europe and the States, put it this way in an interview with *Stylist* magazine: 'For the conversations to be productive, you also have to meet them where they're at and try to understand some of their viewpoints, even if it's uncomfortable.'

Here's what an interactive 'workshop' style looks like, but on the printed page. Think about challenges you might face – as a man, in this case – if you speak up against misogynous behaviour. Whether you are in a school, university, sports, corporate, military or social setting, picture yourself in a situation in which another man in your group has just made a derogatory statement about women. You have to take into account both relational concerns (e.g. *Will I jeopardize my friendship if I say something?*) and ethical considerations (e.g. *If no one else is stepping in, why should I?*).

Next, try to imagine how you would intervene if you chose to do so. Keep in mind that whether you are outgoing or shy, socially assertive or conflict-avoidant, you need to consider numerous other factors that include group norms (e.g. *Do men in this group ever interrupt each other's sexism?*) and many other peer culture dynamics. Have you ever spoken up about these sorts of things in the past? If not, what held you back? If you're white, have you ever challenged a white friend who made a racist comment? Are the ethical considerations any different?

Whether you feel able to have these conversations in your own environment or not, reflecting on these sorts of questions and dynamics is a great place to start. Perhaps you can also think of examples that highlight when you've struggled to speak up in the past. The point of these discussions is to shine a spotlight on one of the key pillars of rape culture that I shared earlier: the silence or active complicity of 'good' men. If you consider yourself one of those men, but struggle with the idea of speaking up in one of these situations, spend some time thinking about why and what steps you might need to take to change that. Perhaps it means going back through some of the earlier points in this book, watching videos like my TEDx Talk on YouTube, or taking a look at some of the other resources I mention in the Notes section at the back of the book. Once we get beyond denial and #NotAllMen defensiveness, it becomes clear that in order to chart a path forward, one of the most transformative things we can do is to change the equation. We need to make it not only 'normal' for men to check each other's sexism – but a sign of their strength and moral integrity.

Ethical Decision-Making

Now that we've thought about some of the barriers to intervening and how important it is to find a way to overcome them, let's turn our attention to what that might look like in practice. The goal is not to come up with the 'right' way to intervene – because there is no right way. There are simply too many unknown variables in any given situation. But by carefully considering the potential implications of your actions on others and yourself, and at the same time hearing how your peers are processing all of this, you'll be in a position to make more ethically conscious decisions.

A useful way to start is to imagine you are in a situation like the one that follows, another hypothetical scenario, or one that you have experienced first-hand. The idea is to bring to mind the responsibilities you have to others, yourself and the group. As a way to illustrate the process, I've included a summary of the trainer's notes for a classic scenario that my colleagues and I often use in workplace trainings. First, read the scenario, and then reflect on the 'train of thought':

SCENARIO
You're out after work having a drink with some male co-workers. One of the guys says something crude and sexually objectifying about a woman who was recently hired in your office. No one says anything.

TRAIN OF THOUGHT
I wish he hadn't just said that. You can't talk about co-workers like that. At the very least it's unprofessional . . . It's also unfair to her and sexist . . . There are no women present, but if no one challenges his statement, aren't we sending the message that it's okay for men to objectify women? . . . She just wants to be treated with respect, and this kind of talk makes that difficult . . . Then again, maybe it's no big deal and I'm overreacting. It's just one statement. And if I say something, it might cause friction in my relationship with him, and we work together . . . What should I do in this situation?

The next step is to consider the following sets of questions about your ethical decision-making process. Remember, there are no right or wrong answers – only a variety of different perspectives, all of which are valuable to think about:

Responsibility to her

In the above scenario, do you, as the bystander, have a responsibility to the woman even if you don't know her? What is the nature of that responsibility? Is it just that she's in a potentially vulnerable spot, and you have a responsibility to her as a fellow human being? Or is it that she's a woman in a sexist society, and it's very difficult for her to be taken seriously as a professional when her male colleagues feel free to sexually objectify her? What if she's a woman of colour and all the men are white? What if they're not?

In MVP trainings, people often say that the bystander has a responsibility to the woman because everyone has worth and dignity. But people don't always speak up and advocate for their fellow humans when that entails some sort of personal risk. We can argue about the nature and extent of that risk. For example, if you don't handle this well, or he reacts poorly, it might cause some lasting awkwardness in your friendship. But if your friend has more seniority or workplace status than you, the repercussions could be more serious. You could lose an opportunity to work on a new project, which in turn might jeopardize your chance of a promotion. Maybe it's still worth taking a risk to say or do something. I don't want to pretend that 'doing the right thing' always comes without consequences, but we need to get better at taking those risks – because if we don't, no one else will, and nothing will change.

Responsibility to him

Do you, the bystander, have a responsibility to the guy who made the comment? If so, why – and if not, why not? Perhaps he might suffer potentially negative repercussions for making those sorts of objectifying comments about women. Maybe what he said is only the tip of the iceberg in terms of his inappropriate conduct around the office. At some point he might get in trouble. He could lose his job. If his friends or colleagues care about *him* and his needs and interests, do they have a responsibility to take him aside and say something?

That conversation can be extraordinarily awkward; just because you work together doesn't mean you've talked honestly about sensitive topics. People who are not skilled interpersonal communicators often avoid unpleasant interactions because they don't know how to approach these subjects with nuance and diplomacy. But the broader question here is about friendship and loyalty, and whether men have a responsibility to each other – and not just to women – to interrupt and challenge misogyny.

Responsibility to oneself

Many people see themselves as the kind of person who takes action in the face of injustice. But in actuality a lot of people don't take action, because real life is usually more messy and complicated than people's fantasies. There are a multitude of reasons why people don't react well in the moment when they're under pressure. So how do they reconcile their self-perception as the kind of person who speaks up with the hard truth with the fact that many times they don't? One way is to tell themselves stories, like *it wouldn't matter anyway*, or *he wouldn't have listened to me*, or *when he's drinking there's no reasoning with him*, or *maybe I was exaggerating, and it really wasn't a big deal in the first place*.

This rhetoric might feel familiar, because we all do it as a way to maintain our self-image, regardless of how we might have acted under pressure. But acknowledging this will help you align your behaviour with your values. By becoming more aware of the reasons you tell yourself that it's okay not to speak up, you're more likely to notice how often you could and should be doing it, and eventually feel more confident to push past those excuses and walk the talk.

Responsibility to the group

Do you, as the bystander, have a responsibility to the group, team, company or some larger entity? If so, what is the nature of that responsibility? Many organizations have a values statement that expresses a spirit of civility and mutual respect: 'We care and look after each other; we work together to bring out the best in ourselves and others.' So when one member of the group treats another with disrespect – for example when a man makes derogatory comments to or about a woman – he's committed a transgression not only against the woman, but against the stated values of the group. This means that a person who calls him on that is not just speaking for himself, i.e. *Yusuf has a problem with what Myles just said*. Rather, everyone on the team/in the workplace has a problem with Myles's comment, and Yusuf was the one who took action. This takes pressure off the individual bystander.

It's worth adding here that in the case of men in groups, a body of research called 'social norms theory' suggests that men often misperceive the extent to which their peers tolerate misogyny or hold rape-supportive attitudes. They might think they're the only one in the group that is bothered by casual expressions of sexism. If so, they're much less likely to say something, especially if the sexist guys are popular or have more status in the group. A bystander is more likely to say something if they know that some of the other guys share their discomfort, because there's safety in numbers. But if no one speaks up, no one ever knows what the others are thinking.

That's why the bystander who speaks up is a leader. Not only is he speaking for himself, he's now become the unofficial spokesperson for the group's values. My colleagues and I have heard countless stories from men who say that when they broke their silence and challenged another man's sexist comment or action, guys thanked them for doing so. They felt a sense of relief that finally (!) somebody said something.

Options

Now that we've given some thought to the ethical questions at hand, let's think about *how* you might act in that situation where a co-worker has said something about a new female co-worker. It's important to consider a range of options, because when people think they only have two choices for intervention in a given situation, and the two choices are either to jump in at the 'point of attack' or do nothing, they often choose to do nothing. The truth is, that's a false set of choices. There are many ways you can make it clear that you're not okay with various types of inappropriate or abusive behaviour. Here are some of the options we include in MVP trainings for the scenario above (the only one we discourage is 'do nothing'):

1. Do nothing. It's not worth getting into a conflict about this.
2. Say something like 'Hey, it's not right to talk about a co-worker like that.'
3. Don't say anything in the group at the moment. But later, find a time when you can talk with him alone, and tell him he really shouldn't talk like that about a co-worker.
4. Talk with a colleague whose judgement you respect and see what they think you should do.
5. Mention to someone in leadership that it would be good to have staff training that addresses how to create and sustain equitable, respectful and healthy work environments – inside and outside the office.
6. Personal option.

The last step in this process is to pick one or more option that you would consider doing. Ask yourself why that one made sense to you, and others didn't. The 'personal option' is included to remind you that your choices are not somehow limited to the ones we've listed.

Further scenarios

Now that you've seen the general structure of scenario/train of thought/options, it's easy to plug in an endless array of possible situations as a way to think about whether, when and how to act. I've included a sampling of scenarios below, followed by condensed trains of thought to kickstart conversations. Consider each one, and then see if you can generate your own list of options.

You're a boy in high school or a young man at university and your friend sends you a nude photo of his ex-girlfriend.

Oh, wow! And oh, no! She would be very upset if she knew he was sharing this. That means she couldn't have consented to it, which is a big problem – and it might even be illegal . . . It can also be emotionally devastating to girls . . . It's not right . . . I wonder if my friend has thought about any of this? Is it my responsibility to let him know this is wrong and that he's got to stop now? . . . Also, I better not forward it to anyone else, because then I'll be guilty too. What should I do?

You play poker with the guys and one of them frequently makes dismissive and hostile comments about his girlfriend and other women, calling them 'whiny bitches' and casually using words like 'sluts' and 'whores'.

This isn't right . . . Guys shouldn't be talking shit about girls like that . . . Sounds like he's got some problems. But what can I say that will make any difference? . . . He might be going through a tough time in his relationship, and he might resent it if he thinks I'm getting in his business . . . Then again, what if this sort of talk is a red flag that he might be abusive to her in private? He's my friend — don't I have some responsibility here? . . . What should I do?

You go drinking and clubbing on the weekends with a group of guys. When you're out, one of them has a habit of grabbing women's butts without warning as they walk by.

I'm embarrassed when my friend acts like this. When he does it I make sure to walk in the other direction, because I don't want women to see me with him . . . Come to think of it, this might actually be sexual assault! . . . So if I keep going out with him, and drinking with him beforehand, aren't I part of the problem? . . . This needs to stop, but what can I say to him? Will he even listen? What should I do in this situation?

You're one of the leaders in a male-dominated organization that places a high premium on brotherhood and loyalty. A woman you know tells you confidentially that her friend was sexually assaulted by one of the guys in the group.

Oh, that's bad news. I'm very sorry to hear about what happened to her friend . . . I'm also sorry to hear that a guy I know was the one who allegedly did it . . . The woman I know confided in me, which means that she trusts I'll handle this with care. But how? Right now it's only an allegation. I don't know the full story . . . One thing I do know is that false reports of sexual assault happen, but they're very rare. And reporting rates are low because women who do report often get a lot of blowback and victim-blaming thrown at them . . . I need to make sure this doesn't happen in my group. We need to respect the rights of both parties . . . But in the meantime, I was told this in confidence, so I have to be very careful about how to proceed. What should I do in this situation?

How You Can Make a Difference

Although these scenarios might seem daunting to read, the act of acknowledging them and our role within them can feel galvanizing. More than thirty years of running bystander and leadership training workshops have shown me that many men find it cathartic and even liberating to talk about the ways in which their fear of being 'unmanned' or ostracized has kept them silently complicit in the face of their fellow men's mistreatment of women. The reality is that many men feel the same and are just waiting for someone else to be an active bystander and break the silence.

Hopefully this chapter has given you some of the tools as well as the permission and confidence to act in line with your moral integrity and have the courage of your convictions. I guarantee you're not the only one who's engaging in this sort of self-reflection. But when you take even a small stand, it gives other men a more positive way to identify with you and each other. This will ultimately contribute to a change in the social acceptability of misogyny, which lies at the root of men's violence against women.

7. What Leaders Can Do

'When a man speaks up and says something, it
breaks the spell and enables all the other good
men with the fairness gene to speak up too.'
– Subha Barry, president, Seramount

'Ending this epidemic of violence has to involve
men stepping up. Because violence against women
is not a problem that women should have to solve.
Men have to be prepared to take responsibility
for our actions and our attitudes. To educate our
sons, to talk to our mates. To drive real change in
the culture of our sporting clubs, our faith and
community groups, and in our workplaces –
including this workplace.'
– Anthony Albanese, prime minister of Australia

From the beginning of this book I've said that *men's*
violence against women is a *men's* issue, and it is. But it's
also more than that. It's a *leadership* issue for men,
whether in the personal realm as a father, godparent,
uncle or mentor, or the professional or educational, as a
coach, teacher, manager, business owner, elected official or countless other positions of influence. This does
not mean that men need to supplant or 'take over'

leadership from women in this space. Far from it. One of the most important things male leaders can do is encourage and promote women's leadership. But men in positions of leadership also need to do whatever they can within their sphere of influence to disrupt the culture of silent complicity in male culture, and become more actively anti-sexist. Not because they're nice guys, but because they're leaders, and we expect that of our leaders. When achieving dramatic reductions in the incidence of gender violence is understood not only as a leadership *issue* but a leadership *imperative* for men, changes in the social norms and institutional practices that sustain misogyny and violence will happen swiftly. The reason is straightforward: male leaders play a vital role in either reinforcing or counteracting those norms and practices. Unfortunately, not enough of them to date have used their stature and influence to do just that.

Command Climate

It should not be up to individual leaders to choose whether or not they think any of this is important and necessary. It should simply be understood as part of the job description for any leadership position, the world over. This is especially true for men in positions of cultural authority and prestige: community leaders, politicians, members of the clergy, business leaders, union officials, sports coaches and league officials, school superintendents, law enforcement officials, judges, university presidents, executive directors of agencies and charities, etc. If they are a man and a leader, this is *their* issue – not a 'women's issue' on which they've generously agreed to help out.

If there has been a shortage of male leaders ready to take on these issues, there has certainly been no shortage of incidents that remind us of the failures of men's leadership. Scandals and preventable tragedies happen as a result of men's violence with alarming regularity. In the summer of 2023, the president of Northwestern University in Chicago fired the popular and accomplished coach of the men's (American) football team after reports emerged of systematic hazing. The incidents involved numerous players in a time period of more than a decade, and included nudity and 'sexual acts of a degrading nature'. The coach – who had been with the team first as a player and then as coach over a period of twenty years – denied that he had known what was going on. Nonetheless, the university president explained his decision by saying that 'the head coach is ultimately responsible for the culture of his team'. In other words, if he didn't know about the abuse, he *should* have.

This is the civilian version of what's known in the military as 'command climate'. In the armed forces, everyone is responsible for their personal behaviour and those beneath them in the chain of command. The commander alone is responsible for everything that goes on under his/her/their command. They're the ones, first and foremost, who set the tone and ensure that the organization's values and standards are upheld. In recent years, one of the most contentious military policy debates in the States has been about one aspect of that responsibility: whether ultimate authority over sexual assault investigations and possible punishments should be in the hands of commanders, or whether decision-making power should rest instead with specialized military prosecutors outside the chain of command.

The UK has seen its share of controversies and scandals about the responsibilities of institutional authorities in cases of sexual misconduct and abuse. One of the most well-known cases boiled over in 2022, when London mayor Sadiq Khan pressured Metropolitan Police commissioner Cressida Dick – the first woman to lead Scotland Yard – to resign amidst growing accusations of deeply rooted and long-standing misogyny and racism in the ranks. One of the particulars concerned a report by a police watchdog office that described a culture of discrimination and harassment in a central London police station, with officers joking about rape and using offensive language in social media posts. The report notably stated that such incidents were part of a wider culture and could not be blamed on 'a few bad apples'.

The Metropolitan Police also came under heavy criticism in 2021 for the aggressive way police handled crowds of (mostly) women protesters who came out after the murder of Sarah Everard by Wayne Couzens, a serving police officer; they eventually agreed to pay compensation to some of the victims. Then attention turned to the internal culture of Britain's largest police service. The *Baroness Casey Review Final Report* on the Met, released in 2023, said that 'Female officers and staff routinely face sexism and misogyny. The Met has not protected its female employees or members of the public from police perpetrators of domestic abuse, nor those who abuse their position for sexual purposes. Despite the Met saying violence against women and girls is a priority, it has been treated differently from "serious violence". In practice, this has meant it has not been taken as seriously in terms of resourcing and prioritization.'

Reports of ineffectual leadership in the face of misogyny and racism in the Met are especially troubling because of the important role played by the police as first responders to gender-based violence, racist hate crimes and other abuses. But the Met is only one organization – however large and high-profile – and law enforcement is only one sector. These types of scandals occur in many other places: business, the military, sports teams, schools. To the extent that recurring problems traceable to 'toxic cultures' have been identified in those institutions, the search for remedies and solutions needs to start at the top.

The Qualities of a Strong Leader

When I conduct gender violence prevention leadership trainings with mixed-gender groups of educational administrators, junior and senior military officers, law enforcement officials or business executives, I often start with an exercise that asks people for one word or phrase that represents a key quality of a strong leader. Many of them have done exercises like this before in generic leadership seminars they've attended. Some have read one or more books about leadership from the thousands that have been published over the years. People raise their hands and offer descriptions like 'decisive', 'compassionate', 'good listener', 'brings out the best in people', 'leads by example', 'proactive rather than reactive', 'has integrity', 'walks the talk', 'serves others', 'courageous'. I write their answers on a whiteboard. When the board is full, I ask the group to come up with explanations for why they think we started the training with this exercise. I usually get a range of thoughtful responses: *Because change starts at the top. Leaders set the tone. We are role models.* My colleagues and I have done this exercise hundreds of times, but only a handful of times has anyone said something about *men's* leadership, and the ways in which it might be part of the solution to the vexing problem of gender-based violence.

By now it might be obvious to someone reading this book, but few people seem to have thought about gender-based violence as a leadership issue for anyone – much less men. Nonetheless, people attend my trainings because they're intrigued by the idea and want to learn new ways of thinking about what leaders can do. What I tell them boils down to this: the qualities leaders need in order to prevent misogynous violence are the same qualities we associate with good leadership in general. The quality I usually highlight is courage, because men's leadership is in short supply on the topic of misogynous violence largely because it often takes a fair degree of courage for a man to interrupt or challenge the sexism of other men. Moral and social courage are required more often than physical courage.

Moral courage can be defined as doing the right thing even when it might come at great personal cost. Its cousin *social courage* involves a willingness to take a risk and say or do something that might be awkward interpersonally, and which if not done with grace and diplomacy might result in a breach of a friendship, or even a loss of status among one's peers.

There is a lot to learn and know about the dynamics of emotional, physical and sexual abuse in and outside of relationships. Accurate, up-to-date information is important – especially about the law. But the reason why men don't speak out or get involved is usually not because they lack the knowledge that something is wrong, or the information about what to do. More likely their failure to act is a result of their doubts, fears and anxieties. Especially their anxieties about what other men – their friends, colleagues and co-workers – will think. In other words, it's more about their hearts than their heads.

When I first began to work with the US Marines I devised a parable to illustrate the difference between physical and moral courage. Imagine that a marine with a reputation for great physical bravery on the battlefield is back home and having a beer with a couple of old friends. One of them tells a crude rape joke. The marine tenses up; maybe his girlfriend is a rape survivor and he's not comfortable laughing about this. But he lets the comment slide. Everyone thinks he's tough and brave and he doesn't want to dent that reputation with a 'politically correct' statement that might come across as virtue-signalling, 'soy boy' behaviour. People might think he's soft! This story prompts the questions: What does it mean to be tough? To be courageous? Does only physical courage count? Isn't moral courage just as worthy of respect?

I discussed this in the previous chapter about

bystanders, but let's make this point again: **if you're a guy, being 'one of the guys' takes nothing special whatsoever**. Going along to get along is not an impressive personal quality. By contrast, it takes a special kind of confidence to turn to your friends who are being disrespectful to women and let them know 'that's not cool'. Any man who has done his time in traditional male environments – especially hyper-competitive subcultures like business or sports – knows this is not easy to do. Which is precisely why it's not very common! It takes a lot more courage to speak up than it does to remain silent. But somehow the guy who speaks up is a wimpy 'beta'? There's something wrong with this picture. Men and young men who interrupt misogyny aren't betas – they're *leaders*, whether they're in an informal or formal environment.

Women's Leadership

As I have noted previously, women's leadership in the movements against gender-based violence has been foundational, transformative and world-changing. Unlike other self-avowed 'leaders', however, many of the activist women in these movements – including large numbers of women of colour – do not identify as leaders in any formal sense. Beginning in the 1970s, women from a diverse range of communities began to organize in response to the widespread problems of domestic abuse and sexual assault. They were especially focused on the needs of women as victims/survivors. Their organizing began in small-scale, grassroots and decentralized networks (e.g.

self-help groups, book clubs, consciousness-raising groups), and later developed into more centralized, formal organizations and government agencies that remain with us to this day. Unfortunately, women at the forefront of these transformational activities rarely receive public acknowledgement for their important contributions.

Since the 1990s, the movement and its allies have taken up the public health model of looking 'upstream' to prevent sexual assault and domestic abuse from occurring in the first place. This has included a growing recognition of the need to engage men in prevention efforts, accompanied by a debate about how to do so in a movement historically created and led by women. As efforts to ramp up men's leadership in this field move forward, it is always important for anti-sexist men to recognize, acknowledge and honour the fact that women created and have long sustained the movements against gender violence. Still, the idea that they are primarily responsible for 'solving' the problem of men's violence unduly burdens the group of people who are its worst victims.

Everyday Leaders

Over the decades, men's leadership on these matters across every sector of society has been sporadic and limited. This is not to say that all men have been missing in action – or that all leadership falls under a narrow definition that requires formal credentials or a highly visible platform. Every day, men all over the world do important and sometimes difficult work in their personal and professional lives to advance gender justice, equity and non-violence. This includes men who mentor women in the workplace, readily acknowledge the contributions of their female colleagues, or perhaps speak up at a meeting when a male colleague takes credit for a woman's idea. It also includes those who provide comfort and assistance to victims and survivors, and engage in compassionate confrontation with abusers. I have worked with countless male social workers, advocates, counsellors and therapists who are deeply committed to their work with victims, survivors and abusers of all genders – and their families – which can be richly rewarding, but also stressful and emotionally exhausting. I've similarly collaborated with multitudes of anti-violence educators in schools, colleges and universities who strive to help their students develop the knowledge and skills not only to be better people and citizens, but also to be part of next-generation, solutions-oriented approaches to the persistent problems of gender inequality and gender violence.

I've also had the good fortune to meet and work with untold numbers of men who just want to help out. These men are often self-effacing and unsung, doing what they know is right or doing their job, not expecting any sort of public recognition for their efforts. The tasks they perform might be as simple as helping to set up the room in a local hall for a fundraising event for a refuge, picking up a guest speaker at the airport, or any one of innumerable large and small acts of solidarity and support for women-led organizations. In my public lectures I often say that I parachute into a community, stride on stage and give a speech from the podium. But it's the women, men and others who work day in and day out in local communities that make a real difference in people's lives, even if they are rarely regarded as leaders.

Unfortunately, over the years of working with large organizations, I have encountered relatively few men in influential positions who see themselves as *anti-sexist* leaders responsible for creative and proactive leadership in gender violence prevention. I suspect this is because until recently this has not really been expected of them. It has been customarily assumed that men's leadership is more likely to be necessary after an incident has occurred. For example, men in law enforcement, along with prosecutors and members of the judiciary, are responsible for the apprehension and punishment of offenders. In the private and non-profit sectors, male CEOs, managers and executive directors (along with women and others in these positions) are responsible for disciplining or firing individuals who violate the company or organization's sexual harassment policy. Other men in positions of cultural influence, such as community leaders or members of the clergy, provide counsel and support to individuals and families who have experienced unimaginable tragedy and loss.

These people deserve credit, respect and gratitude for doing important and often difficult work. But beyond those whose job literally requires them to be immersed in this realm, few men have distinguished themselves as exemplary leaders in the struggle to reduce and eliminate men's violence against women. This is not simply a matter of individual failure. The problem is that, until now, many people have *hoped* male leaders would step up into a more robust and proactive leadership role — but they haven't *expected* it. Alas, transformative change will happen only when men in positions of cultural and political influence understand that leadership is not optional for men in their position, it's in the job description — literally and figuratively.

Men's Leadership in the Public Sphere

It's not just in the workplace or formal organizations that we need better male leaders. There is by now a long list of famous men who have sexually harassed or otherwise assaulted women — or are alleged to have done so. Even before #MeToo, it seemed that anyone who paid attention to the news or social media would regularly hear stories about yet another popular male icon charged with assaulting his wife or girlfriend, or being arrested for sexual assault or the abuse of a child. Sadly, it is much less common to hear about those on the other side of the issue — men who use their platform to speak out against domestic and sexual violence, and the cultural forces that have the effect of normalizing these crimes and abuses.

In media interviews and question-and-answer periods after my talks, people sometimes ask me to name nationally or internationally prominent men who have spoken out or provided a measurable degree of leadership on this global crisis. I can name a few, but the list is short, especially compared to the vast scope of the problem. Many of the men on it are former or current political leaders.

The late South African anti-apartheid icon and president Nelson Mandela gave a speech in 1997 in which he stated that rape, child abuse and domestic violence are not 'problems for women alone to solve', and that while many men do not abuse women and children, the collective voice of these men has never been heard. 'From now on', he said, 'all men will hear the call to assume their responsibility for solving this problem.'

Former American president Jimmy Carter called the mistreatment of women 'the world's number one human rights abuse'. In his 2014 book *A Call to Action: Women, Religion, Violence and Power*, Carter was especially critical of men's leadership in faith communities. Selected scriptures are interpreted, he wrote, 'almost exclusively by powerful male leaders within the Christian, Jewish, Muslim, Hindu, Buddhist, and other faiths, to proclaim the lower status of women and girls. This claim that women are inferior before God spreads to the secular world to justify gross and sustained acts of discrimination and violence against them.'

Barack Obama used the power of his presidency to address the issue of sexual assault on university campuses, and called explicitly on young men to speak out. As a United States senator, former president Joe Biden was a driving force behind the passage of the 1994 Violence Against Women Act, the most sweeping and consequential legislation on this topic in American history. Before he became prime minister, Labour leader Keir Starmer, a former prosecutor and human rights lawyer, asked Britons to 'imagine a society where violence against women is stamped out everywhere', and promised to halve its incidence in ten years. Around the same time, then first minister of Scotland and

Scottish National Party leader Humza Yousaf made an extraordinary statement that should serve as a model for others:

> Whether in politics, in the office, on the worksite, in school, the pub or our own living rooms, we can all do more as men to challenge problematic behaviour among our friends, colleagues and family members. But it is not enough to pontificate and lecture . . . As men, we must listen, we must learn, but we must also demonstrate what a positive male identity looks like to young boys and to other men. Frankly, there is not a grown man in the country today who has not been guilty of problematic behaviour, actions or words towards women in some form. I am no different. Like all men, I have had to reflect on my own behaviour and language over the years. Without doubt, in my younger years I will have told a misogynistic joke at the expense of women, or not challenged behaviour that was demeaning to women. We must ask men to reflect, to be honest and be willing to make the necessary changes in their attitudes, and join a global movement of men who want to stand up and become positive role models for their sons, grandsons, nephews, friends and colleagues.

It is not uncommon for male celebrities to issue statements of outrage and disapproval when men's abusive behaviour is revealed in public, and male athletes around the world have made statements in support of gender justice – whether it's Spanish footballers denouncing the sexism of male leaders toward the women's national team, or, even more courageously, Iranian footballers publicly expressing support for the young women who continue to risk (and lose) their lives in defiance of the deeply misogynous theocrats who run the country.

But the number of well-known and influential men who have stood out as leaders on the issue of gender-based violence is abysmally low, especially when you consider the immediacy and scale of the crisis. Our daily news feeds are filled with stories that range from unbearably tragic cases of domestic homicide to seemingly routine revelations of child sexual abuse scandals in major cultural institutions, not to mention the large-scale sexual violence atrocities that recur in more extreme circumstances like conflict zones and war-torn regions. Long before #MeToo, alarming statistics on the prevalence of domestic and sexual violence had been circulating in media reports and academia for decades, and remain only a click away online.

Where is the sense of urgency and outrage from male leaders about this unnecessary suffering? Why have so few of them been willing to raise their head above the parapet and do something meaningful, especially when it comes to prevention? Where are their impassioned calls to their fellow men, exhorting them to speak up and challenge misogyny when they see it? Of course, there are many reasons why men don't speak up, which I will now outline – not to provide an excuse, but to acknowledge that it's hard to be a leader. Lonely is the head that wears the crown.

The first is that this subject presents especially complicated challenges for leaders of organizations – of all genders – because once an incident has been reported, conflicting narratives emerge, and people take sides. In those instances there is often no way to make a 'popular' decision. In a more general sense, issues of gender and sexual politics can be particularly tricky for male leaders – especially if they're cisgender, self-aware and anti-sexist – because discussions about the dynamics of power and control in relationships, and sexual entitlement, raise many potentially troubling questions regarding matters of privilege and identity. Not to mention that the classic feminist slogan 'the personal is political' applies to men every bit as much as it does to women. Some men do indeed have skeletons in their closets.

At the height of the #MeToo movement, many men – including accomplished and popular leaders – had realistic fears that their past could come back to haunt them, even if they had grown and evolved since earlier periods in their life and might be horrified by what they once considered 'normal' male behaviour. The most outwardly self-confident men sometimes wrestle with their own anxieties and apprehensions around this subject. It's difficult for them to find the 'sweet spot' in which they can express strong disapproval of misogyny and violence and simultaneously avoid adopting a tone of self-righteousness or harsh judgement about *other* men's behaviour.

What makes it especially challenging is that many men have never seen this done successfully by another man. Also, most men know – consciously or not – that if they denounce misogyny and violence with force and clarity, they risk angering and alienating their male friends, colleagues and co-workers. This is a cautionary note for average blokes, but perhaps even more so for men in public life, whose every utterance is open to scrutiny in the era of 24/7 cable TV and social media.

There are reasons why it's still relatively rare – in the twenty-first century! – to hear prominent men speak confidently and forthrightly in public about men's violence against women in anything but the most polite and anodyne language. Many men who see themselves as allies continue to be confused about the role of men's leadership in the post #MeToo era. Should they stay off to the side, listen to women and defer to their greater interest and expertise? Or should they use their powerful voice and lived experience *as men* to set a strong example for other men and boys?

Some other men in high-status positions are undoubtedly resistant to stepping into anti-sexist leadership because they are unrepentant misogynists and would rather cling to old-school ideas about male privilege than bow to 'political correctness' and change with the times. These men have their models. Consider that Donald Trump was elected president of the United States in 2016 despite (or because of) a long public history of misogynous statements and actions, and he remains the most popular figure in the Republican Party to this day. But even many men who are well-meaning and not misogynous often choose to remain silent about all of this, because they are uncomfortable or inarticulate when talking about the loaded issues surrounding gender, sex and power. This is directly analogous to white people who fear they will 'say something wrong' when discussing race, particularly in the presence of people of colour.

The failure of men in positions of political and cultural

leadership to step into this space is surely driven by rational motives and practical considerations such as these. Until it becomes routine and unremarkable for men to talk openly about the responsibility of *every man* to work against misogynous violence, speaking out is likely to be regarded as a reputational or public relations risk for successful men. Especially if they dare to be explicitly critical of other men or beloved parts of male culture that might be implicated as 'part of the problem' (I discussed some of this in the previous chapter).

The positive incentives for this sort of truth-telling are just not there yet – but the negative ones are for sure. Men who denounce men's violence against women are – in a sense – breaking an ancient taboo in patriarchal cultures. They're overtly breaching the 'bro code', which calls for their active participation in sexist rituals, or at least their silent complicity. We know that women who defy sexism do so at great risk – that's why feminism arose in the first place, as a collective response to women's oppression. But this defiance has consequences for men, too. One of those consequences is that some of their fellow men will feel they have thrown men under the bus out of 'woke' self-righteousness, or in order to curry favour with women. From the moment I started writing and speaking about men's violence against women as a university student I regularly heard comments like 'he just wants to get laid' or 'he doesn't really believe that shit' – in retrospect, incredibly mild and innocuous criticisms. In the current era, angry and aggrieved men have access to the tools of social media to amplify their outrage from anonymous accounts, and they pounce on any man who breaks the complicit silence and seeks to hold men – or beloved parts of male culture – accountable in any way.

The outcry is always the same: when you shine a spotlight on the ways in which men either actively or passively contribute to a rape-supportive culture, you're trying to 'blame and shame' men. And because few people realize that you can be 'male-positive' and anti-sexist *at the same time*, as I outlined in chapter 4, men who want and need public support and approval – including from other men – are often reluctant to wade into these waters. There are always exceptions, of course, but one of the main reasons why this is usually the case comes down to this: many male leaders have made the decision – consciously or not – that the 'risks' are simply too great. Let's explore, in brief, some possible explanations for why men in various positions of leadership might be hesitant to run the risk of taking a strong stand on the issue of gender violence.

- Politicians might worry that they'll come off as virtue signallers pandering to women voters with rhetoric they have little intention of backing up with legislative or executive action, especially when they need men's votes.
- Popular artists and entertainers might be leery of raising the ire of their male fans, similar to their caution about taking political stands that could alienate a segment of their audience.
- Professional athletes might have agents and managers who whisper in their ear and warn that publicly identifying themselves with unpleasant and 'controversial' topics like domestic abuse and

sexual assault might raise suspicions about their own history and motives, or come off as awkward and off-putting – which could endanger potentially lucrative sponsorship deals.

- Corporate CEOs might worry about their image as tough, masculine, business-minded leaders if they are overly identified with 'soft' issues coded more as women's concerns. As Ray Arata, founder of the Better Man Conference, says, 'Most men in leadership positions at their companies are engaged in the business, not in the business of engaging men.'

- Even members of the clergy, who are supposed to provide ethical clarity and moral guidance, might be reluctant to challenge men too stridently, especially in an era of declining church attendance and public participation in religious life.

The path of least resistance for all these men – and any other man in a position of cultural or institutional influence – is to either water down their rhetoric and focus on expressions of compassion and care for survivors, publicly decry the most egregious acts of abusers, or keep their head down and avoid the topic entirely. That's why influential men are often silent in public, even if behind the scenes they cheer on the feminist commitments and activities of women close to them, or donate to domestic abuse and sexual assault charities and other women's rights organizations. These actions are admirable, but if they're done in private they do little to disrupt the status quo.

Making Leaders Out of Men

As you can imagine, men's lack of involvement with these issues isn't for the lack of women trying. In fact, on the occasions when they have got involved, it's often been because women have asked, even begged, for their support. Fortunately, some male leaders have answered the call and helped out – as I've seen for myself up close. Over the past several decades, I've taken part in hundreds of campus, community and corporate initiatives that were organized largely by women, but had the backing, support and participation of powerful men. The crucial point is that it was the man's decision – he could either help out or take a pass.

Of course, in an ideal world, women wouldn't even have to ask for men's support on these issues. But in the world in which we find ourselves, the idea of asking men for assistance is wholly inadequate as a model for transformative change. It relies too much on relationships and goodwill. It needs to be replaced by a new model – one in which men's leadership in the area of gender violence prevention does not rely on them being 'good guys' or eager allies, but is understood as a fundamental responsibility they have as *leaders* to address an issue of major seriousness and urgency. This is the focus of my work in schools, with sports teams, and with small and large organizations in the private and public sectors. Creating better leaders holds promise for a more gender-equitable world for future generations. It also has the potential to accelerate change in the present – especially as a means to counter the growing social acceptance of overt expressions of misogyny among men, young men, and boys.

Sometimes an activist educator like me can help by raising expectations for what men can do. Occasionally when I'm scheduled to deliver a guest lecture at a college or university, my hosts arrange for me to meet earlier in the day with a group of campus administrators to talk about sexual assault prevention. Most people who come to these meetings are women, another stark reminder of the gender politics of sexual assault prevention on most campuses – and the low expectations most people have of men in positions of leadership. More than a few times I've attended meetings where not a single man was present, even though my public lectures – which are typically well-publicized events on campus – are explicitly about violence against women as a *men's* issue.

Once, I was in such a meeting at a prestigious liberal arts college in the American Midwest, along with six women and one man. One of the women, a senior administrator, began by asking for my thoughts about working with men on sexual assault prevention. 'This is a real priority for us,' she said. 'We're curious to hear what you have to say.' I asked her what prevention programmes or initiatives were required of students or student leaders. 'We don't have requirements here,' she said. 'We have an "opt-in" campus. We provide students with a range of interesting options for programming and hope they'll take advantage of what we have to offer.' But hadn't she said a moment earlier that sexual assault prevention was a priority for them? How could it be a priority if students – including the male students who commit the vast majority of reported sexual assaults – could choose whether or not they wanted to be involved?

The tension between optional and mandatory sexual assault prevention programming on college or university campuses offers a small window into a much larger challenge that has bedevilled sexual assault activists and educators for at least two generations – how to get men to take this stuff seriously. Since the 1990s, women in the GBV movements have discussed and debated ways to get more men through the door at various events they organize. But sadly, it almost always comes down to this: if it's 'optional' for men to participate, few of them will.

I have a unique perspective on these processes, because I have visited many hundreds of communities all over North America (and elsewhere) as the 'headliner' for events specifically designed to attract men. Almost every one of these instances is initiated by women leaders of domestic abuse, sexual assault and anti-human-trafficking organizations who want to engage men but often have limited tools to work with. A common scenario is when a charismatic executive director of a refuge or sexual assault agency invites prominent men in the community to a talk or training, and they can't say no. I've heard all sorts of creative strategies women have devised to get men to show up. Free food and drink (free beer?). A raffle featuring prizes like four tickets to a football match in a luxury box accompanied by a retired Hall of Fame player. Whatever gets them through the door.

In the early 2000s I played a role in the development of a new and promising model for how to engage men. The idea was to have early morning leadership gatherings – *Breakfast with the Guys!* – that were designed to bring together local male leaders in business, politics, sports, education, law enforcement, etc. The breakfasts, which were typically organized by feminist community leaders, had two main goals: to generate broader support for local domestic and sexual abuse programmes, and to discuss ways in which local male leaders could provide strong anti-sexist leadership within their sphere of influence. They were often co-chaired by prominent retired male athletes or coaches in order to send a message to men that it was okay for them to attend, and ease their anxiety about showing up at a 'women's event'.

I met many strong and compassionate men at these events, some of whom were looking for concrete suggestions about what more they could do, both in their role in the community and as fathers and adult men who felt a sense of responsibility to young people. But for all its appeal, this organizing model depends too heavily on the time and hard work of women in domestic abuse and sexual assault organizations, and not enough on work from men in the community. What's more, it's a model for 'engaging men' that is still voluntary. Men can choose whether or not to attend.

But even with that limitation, it still holds promise as a mode of organizing. As I've said, some men who attend these types of events say they are willing to do more – if asked. So, let's ask the question: why don't some of you men who are reading this decide to take the initiative and organize one of these community leadership breakfasts with some friends and colleagues, and in consultation with local women's organizations?

Informal Leaders

Leadership isn't always formal. Opportunities for leadership also occur frequently in friendship, peer culture and workplace settings in which men and young men find themselves. For example, let's imagine that one boy in a group of seventeen-year-old boys – let's call him Oliver – constantly texts his girlfriend, eager to know what she's wearing, who she's with and other details of her daily life. The other boys sense this is unhealthy but nobody says or does anything. Then one day, one of the guys in the group – let's call him Tom – takes Oliver aside and tells him he's concerned. 'I'm worried about you and your girlfriend,' he says. 'You seem to be really jealous or something. Is everything okay?' Tom might not think of himself as a leader, but he has just executed a basic leadership protocol. He's identified a problem (controlling behaviour of this sort is harmful by itself, and could be an indication of or precursor to more severe forms of coercive control), reflected upon his responsibilities to the various parties (the girlfriend, perhaps other girls/women he knows who've experienced abuse in relationships, his friend, his own values, etc.), considered a set of options ('what can I do now?'), selected one and then acted. People in formal positions of leadership do this all the time. But when you define leadership more broadly like this, formal credentials are unnecessary.

Anyone can be a leader. Average guys can speak up and interrupt misogynous banter from their mates and help to set an anti-sexist tone in their friendship circles, teams, workplaces and other peer cultures – even if they're not already recognizable leaders in the group. (This is the heart of the bystander approach.) It's not an easy thing to do, which is precisely why it doesn't happen too often. Describing it as an act of leadership has the added feature of being positive and aspirational. You're 'calling in' young men to be strong voices for fairness and justice, not calling them out as toxic males and misogynists. It also provides a shield against possible attacks from male peers who might question the 'manhood' of young men who 'stand with women' or take the side of feminists in criticizing casual misogyny and other features of rape culture.

Such taunting is especially virulent on social media, where men who criticize other men's sexist treatment of women open themselves up to mockery and ridicule for being 'betas' and 'cucks' – two of the worst things you can call socially and sexually insecure young men. The dynamic is even more pronounced in influential, male-dominated subcultures like sports, law enforcement, the military and certain sectors of the business world, where hierarchy is rigidly enforced and members feel great pressure to conform to group norms – or suffer the consequences. The irony, of course, is that a young man (or old) who makes it clear that he disapproves of comments by his friends or peers that degrade women is displaying courage and leadership – and is thus precisely the opposite of a weak beta.

How to be a Better Leader

As we've seen, anti-sexist men's leadership is in short supply around the world largely because it's voluntary – and not enough men have signed up. The good news is that there's a relatively straightforward solution. First, we need to describe men and young men who speak out about sexism as *leaders* – whether or not they occupy formal positions of leadership. Second, we need to make gender violence prevention leadership training mandatory for those in power – and organically build it into normative mentoring and educational processes for anyone who wants to advance their education or career.

We can all agree – or at least most of us can – that sexual harassment, sexual assault and domestic abuse are enormous problems that cause untold human suffering, do grievous harm to children, cost many billions of pounds per year in health expenses, and contribute to a wide range of social ills. Leaders have disproportionate status and authority, and thus bear a disproportionate share of the burden for preventing it from happening. Spider-Man's uncle said it best: with great power comes great responsibility.

We can't expect male leaders across multiple sectors to be experts on the subject. But it's not necessary that they are. As I have said throughout this book, men in positions of leadership can do a great deal to change the social norms in male culture that actively or tacitly condone misogynous abuse. By definition, leaders exert disproportionate influence in their domain. We need them to wield this influence in a way that helps to create a climate *among men* in which misogynous attitudes and behaviour are seen as out of step with prevailing sentiments and completely unacceptable to all members of the group.

Leaders can bring their unique talents to bear in all the ways in which they exercise leadership. But the knowledge and skills they need to fulfil their responsibilities around the prevention of gender-based violence fall into three discrete areas. Whatever the size and scope of their sphere of influence, anti-sexist leaders need to:

1) **Support** victims and survivors, and work to foster an environment in which they are respected and supported.

2) **Interrupt the enactment of abuse, and hold harassers and abusers accountable,** by reinforcing social norms around respectful, non-sexist behaviour, but also by enforcing laws, codes, policies and anti-discrimination guidelines.

3) **Exercise proactive leadership** in order to create and sustain a group environment in which misogynous abuse – and all forms of disrespectful behaviour – is seen as socially unacceptable and contrary to the group's shared values.

Imagine how much more quickly things could change if it was mandatory for everyone of all genders who wished to ascend the ranks of leadership – from youth sports team captains to CEOs of major corporations – to receive training that helps them acquire some working knowledge about gender-based violence and develop the skills to complete the three basic leadership responsibilities listed above.

Imagine if all men – young and old – who aspire to be leaders were required to do this. The requirement would get them through the door. But what they would learn once they walked through that door would help to increase exponentially the number of men who become strong anti-sexist leaders – and allies to women and non-binary people – in the long struggle to reduce and eliminate gender-based violence.

How You Can Make a Difference

The beauty of defining gender violence prevention as a leadership issue is that anyone can be a leader. The young man who takes his friend aside to express concern about the way the friend treats his girlfriend is not just an *active bystander*. He is a *leader*. The reason why it's so powerful to reframe gender violence prevention as a leadership issue – especially for men – is that it's positive and aspirational. It gives men who see themselves as 'good guys' a way to move beyond defensiveness and make a meaningful contribution to change. But it will truly be a game-changer when leadership training on this topic becomes a requirement for leaders or aspiring leaders at all levels of cultural, institutional and political authority and power.

8. Where Do We Go from Here?

There's a time for analysis and a time for action. Both are vitally necessary, but now's the time for 'action'. As I've said throughout this book, men on the whole have not yet met the moment in the struggle to end gender-based violence. The good news is we have it in our power to change that.

One of the more hopeful developments that resulted from the horrific murder of Sarah Everard in 2021, and the ensuing upsurge in women's activism, was that many men said they wanted to know what they could do. I'll repeat now what I said then. You don't need to start from scratch; the foundation has already been built. But there is a world of possibilities. What's been missing has not been a failure of imagination, but a failure of will. Men who are ready to move beyond the reactive posturing of #NotAll-Men can make an enormous difference.

Many years ago, when my colleagues and I first began to do gender violence prevention work with male university athletes, we could sense the defensiveness many of them felt about this subject. They were painfully aware of the unflattering stereotypes many people held of them as loutish and entitled, especially with regard to their treatment of women. I told them – and tell other men who feel similarly misunderstood or disrespected – that they had to make a choice. They could hunker down in a defensive crouch and complain about being maligned or unfairly judged. Or they could do something proactive and constructive to prove the doubters wrong. Don't cry #NotAllMen and seek absolution. Instead, *show* them that not all men are – or want to be – part of a system that does incalculable harm to women and girls.

I want this final chapter to be ambitious and goal-oriented, so in the spirit of 'go big or go home' I've outlined a series of action steps men can take – at the personal, cultural, institutional and political levels. The list isn't comprehensive – opportunities for constructive action are almost limitless. But my assumption is that anyone who has read this far will likely welcome further suggestions about what they can do to make a difference. Not coincidentally, in my gender violence prevention leadership trainings, the final module we do is an exercise where the participants break into small groups and are asked to generate a list of 3–5 action steps they plan to take. Of course, there's no guarantee that anyone will follow through with any of them. But there is something about laying out hopes and aspirations in 'to do' lists that makes them seem . . . doable.

A personal note of interest: the action steps listed below are an updated and expanded version of a document I produced around 1990 entitled 'Ten Things Men Can Do to Prevent Gender Violence'. It started out as a paper flyer that I and my fellow activists would distribute to people *by hand* at rallies, marches, sports events and various creative venues, and that university professors and others posted on bulletin boards, office doors and other brick and mortar structures. When the internet took off in the mid-1990s, it quickly began to circulate around the world.

By now it's undergone several iterations and has been translated into numerous languages.

What Can Men Do?

What specific steps can men take? I've compiled the following list of action items based on my own work and research, input from my colleagues in the anti-violence movement, and feedback and suggestions I've received along the way. It's arranged in a rough progression from the personal, to the institutional, to the political. It's neither a comprehensive nor a static list. Rather, I'd like to think of it as a dynamic document that can grow at any time or be amended as necessary. And there's one more thing. For anyone who is task-driven and mission-oriented – which includes a lot of men who have made it through this book but are still new to all of this – consider the list a blueprint for action. But doing the work is up to you.

21 Action Steps for Men

1. Have the Courage to Look Inward

It's easy for 'good men' men to blame other men for behaving badly. But truly transformative work starts with looking inward. Question your own attitudes about gender, sex and entitlement. Try hard to understand how your own behaviours might inadvertently perpetuate misogyny and violence, and work toward changing them.

Try not to be overly defensive when something you say or do ends up hurting or offending someone else.

2. Ask if You Can Help

If you suspect that a woman (or anyone else) close to you is being abused or has been sexually harassed or assaulted, gently ask if you can help. Be supportive and non-judgemental. Get information about options from local women's organizations or national hotlines and share them with her, but don't expect to 'fix' the situation.

3. Speak Up

If a friend, classmate, teammate, co-worker or colleague is abusing his female partner – or is disrespectful or abusive to girls and women in general – don't look the other way. If you feel comfortable doing so, try to talk to him about it. Urge him to seek help. If you don't know what to do, seek advice and support from a trusted friend, mentor or workmate. Don't remain silent and complicit.

4. Get Help

If you are emotionally, psychologically, physically or sexually abusive to women, or have been in the past, seek therapy, counselling or some other professional assistance now. Asking for help is an act of integrity and not a sign of weakness; in fact, it often requires great personal courage. If you come from a family with a history of abuse and trauma, getting help to stop yourself from passing down the pain is a precious gift to your children and future generations.

5. Educate Yourself

Seek out some of the voluminous writing and research by women over the past generation about gender inequality, misogyny and the root causes of all forms of GBV. In addition, check out the burgeoning literature about multi-cultural masculinities and violence. Watch TED Talks, TikToks and YouTube videos on issues related to gender and violence. Listen to podcasts, attend programmes, take courses, watch documentary films, and read articles and books about sexual assault and related topics. Read *Voice Male* magazine. Browse through the library of resources at XYOnline.net, or Equimundo.org. Educate yourself and others about the ways in which personal problems and relational conflicts are often rooted in larger systemic injustices.

6. Show Up

One of the most important things people can do is *show up* for causes about which they care. Alas, relatively few men have demonstrated that care when it comes to men's violence against women. Most of the people who attend protests about GBV are women, as are most of the participants in meetings on the subject at school and in the workplace. Sometimes the most important message men need to send is the one they deliver by their presence.

7. Join the Cause

Be an ally to women, non-binary people, and others from marginalized identities who are working to end all forms of gender violence. Support their organizing efforts. Attend Reclaim the Night rallies and other public events. Volunteer to help set up or clean up. If you're a member of a local civic organization, raise money for community-based rape crisis centres and domestic abuse refuges. If you're part of a student group, organize a fundraiser to raise money for those programmes, and spread awareness among your fellow students.

8. Make the Connection

Recognize and speak out against violence toward transgender, non-binary and genderqueer people, the majority of which is perpetrated by men. Of course, discrimination and violence against LGBTQ people are wrong in and of themselves. But this abuse also has direct links to sexism, because men with 'hostile sexist' attitudes toward women often question the 'manhood' and heteronormativity of men who speak out against sexism, which is a conscious or unconscious strategy intended to intimidate and silence them.

9. Make Sure Your GBV Prevention Work is Culturally Sensitive

Misogynous abuse and violence occur in every culture, but the solutions we employ can never be one-size-fits-all.

Action plans to counteract gender-based violence in diverse twenty-first-century societies need to account for racial, ethnic and religious differences. White men especially need to support and amplify – whenever possible – the voices of people of colour who work to end sexist violence within their communities and in the larger society.

10. Be a Critic of Misogyny in Media

Misogynous media doesn't *cause* men's violence against women – but it normalizes it and desensitizes viewers/listeners to its brutality. When you see portrayals of women in entertainment media that reinforce harmful misogynous myths and stereotypes, find ways to speak out against them. Make the choice not to spend money on entertainment that perpetuates sexist and/or racist stereotypes and degrades women, whether in films, porn, TV, music, comedy, advertising, video games or other forms of media. If you are an educator, parent or mentor, provide or promote media literacy education for young people that shines a critical spotlight on misogynous media.

11. Refuse to Participate in Online Misogyny

Digital technology is responsible for phenomenal advances, but it has also facilitated disturbing new forms of misogynous abuse. Men who care about gender justice and basic human decency have a choice to make: they can either join in and thus support the perpetuation and spread of online misogyny, quietly decline to participate, or denounce it and work to make it socially unacceptable.

Online abuse includes the overt and egregious misogyny in the manosphere, but it also includes expressions of casual misogyny on social media platforms like Instagram, Snapchat, TikTok, Facebook, Twitter, Tumblr and Reddit. Sexualized bullying against women – and increasingly, overt threats against them, including cyber-stalking – is so prevalent in parts of the online world that many girls and women feel unsafe going there. Men need to call out misogynous abuse online when they see it, for example by impressing on their friends that sharing non-consensual intimate images (NCIIs) is never okay. Nor is it ever okay or just 'edgy' fun to use rapidly proliferating technologies, such as AI-generated non-consensual deepfake porn, to harass or punish women (or anyone).

12. Say No to Commercial Sexual Exploitation

The porn industry, strip clubs, paid sex and sex trafficking would not exist without demand. Don't be one of the 'nice guys' who just wants a little fun and doesn't want to think about the harms you might be perpetuating. Always remember that it is not 'anti-sex' to oppose sexual exploitation in its various forms. It is anti-violence and anti-oppression.

13. Promote Sex Education

The porn industry remains the world's largest source of sex education for boys and men (as well as girls, women and non-binary individuals). Parents and other adults have a responsibility to counteract the abusive and distorted picture of sexuality young people get from it by supporting and lobbying for comprehensive, porn-critical sex education. In particular, fathers and other adult men need to raise their voices and join the growing women-led movement to address the proliferation of misogynous porn as a global public health crisis.

14. Support, Join and Create Anti-Sexist Men's Organizations

Volunteer to work with anti-sexist men's programmes such as Beyond Equality, Men at Work, the White Ribbon Campaign, the Men's Development Network (Ireland), A Call to Men (US), Next Gen Men (Canada), Men Against Violence and Abuse (India), Sonke Gender Justice (South Africa) and MÄN (Sweden). If you work in a large organization, join or create an anti-sexist men's caucus. Contact the MenEngage Alliance, a multi-country network of NGOs, UN agencies and other organizations that work with men on issues of gender violence, fatherhood, caregiving and other men's issues.

15. Be Accountable

We need more men to join the struggle against gender-based violence. But they need to do it with sensitivity and respect, because women have been at this for a very long time. Men who speak up or speak out – either as individuals or in groups – should certainly be bold and take the initiative. Nonetheless, they should be in dialogue with women along the way, and also have some meaningful degree of formal and informal accountability to women's organizations that have long been the leaders on all of this.

16. Raise the Issue in Other Movements

Sexual harassment and assault are problems even within movements dedicated to equity and justice. If you are a man in these movements, support women who are trying to raise the issue internally, and do what you can to organize other men. Also, it is important that people involved in work on the housing crisis, anti-racism, knife crime, gang violence, climate change, etc. are aware of the many ways in which gender inequality and gender-based violence intersect and overlap with those issues. If you're part of these movements, or know people who are, urge people to educate themselves and others on the connections and incorporate gender violence prevention into activist efforts.

17. Wealthy Men: Fund Initiatives

Many anti-sexist initiatives that work with men, young men, and boys are underfunded and understaffed, and therefore hampered in their ability to reach large numbers of people with educational outreach programmes, public campaigns, and other means to shape popular consciousness and change social norms. Government funding is important but often limited. Men (and women) with philanthropic resources can make an enormous difference virtually overnight – locally, nationally and globally. Many effective but small and/or local initiatives need funding to scale up. Among many other things, they need resources to create a more robust social media presence that can help to counteract the pervasive misogyny found online. Wealthy men can make that happen and accelerate the pace of change.

18. Use Your Leadership Platform

If you're a man in a position of community, institutional, political or business leadership, do whatever you can within your sphere of influence to create and sustain an environment in which misogynous behaviour is completely unacceptable. Don't wait for incidents to occur and then react. Instead, make an effort to institute policies and initiate conversations about gender violence prevention with your staff, employees, team members, constituents, etc. If you're part of an educational institution, registered charity or private business, make gender violence prevention leadership training mandatory for junior and senior administrators, leaders and managers.

19. Denounce Violence Against Women in Politics

Politicians of all genders face increased personal scrutiny and pressure from a rising tide of right-wing populist anger directed toward governing elites, but women in politics are especially vulnerable – especially women who deviate from gender norms or are explicitly feminist. One of the special threats these women face is violence from men – whether expressed in hostile and abusive comments online, or in more specific and tangible threats that attract the attention of law enforcement. Men who not only abhor violence but also believe in 'playing by the rules' need to find a stronger voice on this issue. They can start by pushing back against the idea that violent rhetoric in politics is normal, and that the problem is not gendered because male political leaders are also sometimes targeted.

20. Implement the Istanbul Convention

It's the law. In 2022, the UK ratified the Istanbul Convention, Europe's first legally binding instrument on violence against women. The Convention defines such violence as discrimination and a human rights violation, and obliges states to undertake comprehensive legal and practical measures that offer a 'holistic response'. Article 12 states that 'parties shall take the necessary measures to promote changes in the social and cultural patterns of behaviour of women and men with a view to eradicating prejudices, customs, traditions and all other practices which are based on the idea of the inferiority of women or on stereotyped roles for women and men.' It also provides explicit guidance to political leaders that reflects a growing consensus about prevention: 'Parties shall take the necessary measures to encourage all members of society, especially men and boys, to contribute actively to preventing all forms of violence covered by the scope of this Convention.'

21. Mentor Others

If you're a father, grandfather, uncle or mentor to boys and young men, teach them how to be men in ways that don't involve degrading or abusing girls and women (or anyone). Don't be afraid to acknowledge that you don't have all the answers. Seek support from other men in your life who have similar concerns. Go online and get information and ideas from organizations like Equimundo that do research on fatherhood and the role of other adult men in the lives of children. Lead by example.

Strong Men

Anti-sexist men routinely hear from people who think we're trying to make men soft and weak. 'We need men to be strong,' they say. 'The problem in our society isn't too much masculinity, it's too little!' Those voices have grown louder in recent years on both sides of the Atlantic, in part as a backlash to the growing demand from women – especially young women – to be treated with respect in cultures awash in misogyny and violence.

They're right about one thing – we do need men to be strong. But the critical issue isn't whether it's good for men to be strong; it's how we define strength. Is it measured primarily in crude physical terms, as the ability to impose your will on others through force and displays of dominance? Really? Is that how we're supposed to define masculine strength in the twenty-first century? I prefer a much more expansive definition, one that includes the qualities of moral and social courage, an unrelenting commitment to the pursuit of justice, and a willingness to take risks in your personal or professional life to interrupt abuse – and, whenever possible, relieve the suffering of others.

As I've recounted in these pages, millions of men support

women and girls in their struggles against misogyny and violence. But most often they do so quietly and in private. That's not to say it's unimportant; it can even be heroic. But not nearly enough men have used the tools available to us within our spheres of influence to catalyse change at the scale required for broader social transformation. To date, men's collective response to the ongoing crisis of men's violence against women has been woefully inadequate. We've got a long way to go before we achieve a critical mass of men – across a racially and ethnically broad and diverse coalition around the world – that can join with women to create a tipping point in the historic movements to end all forms of misogynous abuse. But the very publication of this book suggests that progress is possible. And as generations change, so too will the look and face of the people engaged in the struggle.

The journalist and feminist campaigner Julie Bindel writes that back in the 1980s, the men against sexism she met were all of a type: 'bearded vegans who carried babies in a papoose and knitted or crocheted, rather than going to the pub or playing football'. (She hadn't met me and many of my colleagues.) She emphasizes that many of the men she did meet were and remain valuable allies, but a new generation of anti-sexist men disrupts the old clichés. 'They do not look one way, nor do they necessarily sign up to a particular ideology, although they share a commitment to social equality. They simply want to get things done. This is a new wave of men, creating a movement that fits with the context of today.'

Individual action is important, and this book provides a road map for men who want to go on that journey. But of course real sustainable change requires policy and institutional change as well. 'In a world where women face persistent, structural barriers to equality,' says Gary Barker, president and CEO of Equimundo, 'having more men calling out other men for harmful behaviour is urgent and necessary, but far from sufficient. We have to realize that without systemic change, we won't get systemic results.'

It is widely acknowledged that many men today are hurting – especially young men. They face multiple challenges: an epidemic of loneliness, mental health problems, drug addiction, increasing economic anxiety and insecurity, not to mention looming environmental and climate catastrophes. Amidst all of this, a consensus is growing that one of their greatest problems is a crisis of connection and meaning. As we've seen, all too often these men have been taken in by political demagogues and manipulative charlatans, who blame strong women for men's problems, and urge men to double down on their control of women in order somehow to make themselves feel better or bolster their feelings of lost glory. But as I've maintained throughout this book, it's not only possible to address men's needs at the same time as we push them to work against sexism – it's imperative. The issues are inextricably interwoven.

Those of us who care about men, but want to see much less misogyny and violence in the world, need to reach them with a more aspirational story about masculinity. It's one in which manhood is a form of moral selfhood. It's based on fundamental concepts of fairness and human rights. It's a vision of masculinity that will benefit women, but it will also improve men's lives and relationships immeasurably – with people of all genders. It's one in which men stand with women, LGBTQ people, and anyone who wants to be treated with dignity and respect. It's one in which we call men in to become part of the historic struggle for equality and justice.

Acknowledgements

Writing is a solitary act, but this book is based on work that is anything but. In fact, I have always seen myself as part of a *movement* – the multiracial movement to end gender-based violence – that is one of the most consequential anti-violence movements in history. Because of this, I have had the great good fortune to work with many incredible friends and colleagues in my own country, but also in the UK and around the world.

I want to thank all the women in the movement who have welcomed and encouraged me and my work over many years. I will forever be in your debt. I am grateful as well to my fellow men in the movement for their ongoing solidarity and friendship.

I can't possibly thank everyone by name who has contributed to my work over the time I've been writing this book. Family, friends and fellow activists who sustained me personally or provided professional camaraderie, and sometimes both, include: David Levy, Gail Dines, Byron Hurt, Rob Okun, Adi Bemak, Shelley Eriksen, Andrew and Susan Bellak, Diane Rosenfeld, Ashley Judd, Don McPherson, Carrie Baker, Jan Bue, Dan Miller, Dode Levenson, Jeremy Earp, Loretta Alper, Rivka Polatnick, Jean Kilbourne, Miriam Zoll, Alan Heisterkamp, Graham Goulden, Sandra Holstein, Debby Tucker, Linda and Larry Fryer, Michael Ash, Leah Aldridge, Janet Miller, Maria and Steve Heim, Jennifer

Siebel Newsom, Caroline Heldman, Gary Barker, Alex and Susan Prout, John Badalament, Elizabeth Ziegler, Dylan Hays, Tom Keith, Mark Mlawer, Tom Digby, Wendy Marsden, Robin Kurka, Kevin MacRae, Melissa Perry, David Cain, Harish Sadani and Altamash Khan. Special gratitude for the friendship and support I've received from members of my Sunset-Lincoln crowd.

Thanks as well to old friends and newer acquaintances on Facebook, LinkedIn and Instagram, who have been an important resource for information and real-time feedback, as well as an ongoing source of community and connection in this beautiful and broken world.

I also want to give a shout-out to all of my MVP colleagues, past and present. MVP has blessed me with lifelong friendships and afforded me the opportunity to work with many exceptional colleagues and fellow trainers over the years. Special thanks to Rich Lapchick and the late Art Taylor for greenlighting the initial project at Northeastern University's Center for the Study of Sport in Society more than thirty years ago!

No acknowledgements section would be complete – and honest – without a shout-out to the academics, journalists and writers whose work I draw on in these pages. The gold standard of researcher-activists is Michael Flood, who deserves special thanks for the treasure trove of resources he generates and curates at his invaluable website XYonline.net. Thanks as well to Sandy Ruxton and Stephen Burrell, whose fantastic podcast *Now and Men* is a UK-based global resource for people doing pro-feminist work in academic and non-academic settings. Thanks also to the folks at Equimundo, the source of groundbreaking global reports about men and masculinities that I use regularly in my writing and speaking.

A number of people reviewed portions of the manuscript and gave me valuable feedback at various junctures: David Levy, Leah Aldridge, Rob Okun, La Shonda Coleman, Judah Katz, Ninu Kang and David Cain. The book is better because of their contributions, but of course I take full responsibility for anything that might have fallen short on accuracy or impact.

Thanks for the work of my literary agent, Jim Levine at Levine, Greenberg, Rostan in New York, and his partners at Abner Stein in London. I am grateful to my editors at Penguin, all of whom are women, and all of whom played critical roles in guiding this project to fruition. Props to Emily Robertson, who heard a podcast interview I did with the *Guardian* after Sarah Everard's murder and was determined to find a way to bring my writing to a UK audience. I then went to work with Amy McWalters to fashion a manuscript that did justice to the depth and complexity of this subject, but in a way that would be relatable to a broad audience – especially men. Thanks, Amy, for bucking conventional wisdom in your industry by believing this was possible – and then skilfully seeing it through to the end. Thanks to Celia Buzuk for her expert work in streamlining the narrative, bringing clarity and focus to the final piece, and to Gemma Wain for her fantastic copy-editing contributions.

I also want to take this opportunity to express my appreciation and gratitude for the many British writers and artists – especially the bands formerly known as The

Quarrymen and The Detours – whose words and music have given this American untold joy and inspiration, from childhood right up to the present.

Finally, I want to give special thanks to my son Judah for being such a good sport, sounding board, and source of care and support over the long march of this book's journey to completion. And to Shelley, much gratitude and love for all you do and have done for me, side by side in life and work all these many years.

Bibliography

Adichie, Chimamanda Ngozi, *We Should All Be Feminists*, Anchor Books, 2014.

Bancroft, Lundy, *Why Does He Do That? Inside the Minds of Angry and Controlling Men*, Berkley Books, 2003.

Bates, Laura, *Men Who Hate Women: From Incels to Pickup Artists, the Truth About Extreme Misogyny and How It Affects Us All*, Simon & Schuster, 2020.

Courtenay, Will, *Dying to be Men: Psychosocial, Environmental, and Biobehavioral Directions in Promoting the Health of Men and Boys*, Routledge, 2011.

Dines, Gail, *Pornland: How Porn Has Hijacked Our Sexuality*, Beacon Press, 2010.

Flood, Michael, *Engaging Men and Boys in Violence Prevention (Global Masculinities)*, Palgrave Macmillan, 2019.

Gilligan, James, *Violence: Reflections on a National Epidemic*, Putnam, 1996.

Herman, Judith L., *Truth and Repair: How Trauma Survivors Envision Justice*, Basic Books, 2023.

hooks, bell, *The Will to Change: Men, Masculinity, and Love*, Washington Square Press, 2004.

Jensen, Robert, *Getting Off: Pornography and the End of Masculinity*, South End Press, 2007.

Johnson, Allan, *The Gender Knot: Unraveling Our Patriarchal Legacy*, Temple University Press, 1997, 2014.

Katz, Jackson, *The Macho Paradox: Why Some Men Hurt Women and How All Men Can Help*, Sourcebooks, 2006; revised edition 2019.

Kaufman, Michael, *The Time Has Come: Why Men Must Join the Gender Equality Revolution*, Counterpoint, 2019.

Kaur, Jaspreet, *Brown Girl Like Me: The Essential Guidebook and Manifesto for South Asian Girls and Women*, Bluebird, 2022.

Kimmel, Michael, *Guyland: The Perilous World Where Boys Become Men*, Harper, 2008.

Manne, Kate, *Down Girl: The Logic of Misogyny*, Oxford University Press, 2018.

McPherson, Don, *You Throw Like a Girl: The Blind Spot of Masculinity*, Akashic Books, 2019.

Messner, Michael, et al., *Some Men: Feminist Allies and the Movement to End Violence Against Women*, Oxford University Press, 2015.

Mill, John Stuart, *The Subjection of Women*, Dover, 1997 (first published in London by Longmans, Green and Company, 1869).

Okun, Rob, ed., *Voice Male: The Untold Story of the Profeminist Men's Movement*, Interlink, 2014.

Orenstein, Peggy, *Boys & Sex: Young Men on Hookups, Love, Porn, Consent, and Navigating the New Masculinity*, Harper, 2020.

Perry, Kennetta Hammond, *London is the Place for Me: Black Britons, Citizenship and the Politics of Race*, Oxford University Press, 2015.

Plank, Liz, *For the Love of Men: From Toxic to a More Mindful Masculinity*, St. Martin's Press, 2019.

Pollack, William, *Real Boys: Rescuing Our Sons from the Myths of Boyhood*, Henry Holt, 1998.

Real, Terrence, *I Don't Want to Talk About It: Overcoming the Secret Legacy of Male Depression*, Scribner, 1997.

Reeves, Richard, *Of Boys and Men: Why the Modern Male Is Struggling, Why It Matters, and What to Do About It*, Brookings, 2022.

Rosenfeld, Diane, *The Bonobo Sisterhood: Revolution Through Female Alliance*, Harper Wave, 2022.

Ross, Loretta, *Calling In: How to Start Making Change with Those You'd Rather Cancel*, Simon & Schuster, 2025.

Smith, David G., and W. Brad Johnson, *Good Guys: How Men Can Be Better Allies for Women in the Workplace*, Harvard Business Review Press, 2020.

Snyder, Rachel Louise, *No Visible Bruises: What We Don't Know About Domestic Violence Can Kill Us*, Bloomsbury, 2019.

Van de Kolk, Bessel, *The Body Keeps the Score: Brain, Mind, and Body in the Healing of Trauma*, Penguin Books Ltd, 2014.

Way, Niobe, *Rebels with a Cause: Reimagining Boys, Ourselves, and Our Culture*, Dutton, 2024.

Westmarland, Nicole, et al., *Men's Activism to End Violence Against Women: Voices from Spain, Sweden and the UK*, Policy Press, 2021.

Whippman, Ruth, *BoyMom: Reimagining Boyhood in the Age of Impossible Masculinity*, Harmony, 2024.

Notes

Introduction

p. 1, *The feeling was widespread*: Indian women expressed similar sentiments after the brutal gang rape and murder of twenty-three-year-old Jyoti Singh and the assault of her male companion by a group of young men on a private bus in New Delhi in 2012. The attack on the young woman, who came to be known as Nirbhaya ('the fearless one'), sparked nationwide protests among women (and men) outraged by societal inaction about gender-based violence. In Ireland on 12 January 2022, the brutal murder of twenty-three year-old Ashling Murphy, a primary school teacher and traditional Irish musician who was out for a jog, prompted similar nationwide expressions of shock and grief, and an outpouring of outrage about men's violence against women. Thirty-one-year-old Jozef Puska, an immigrant from Slovakia and father of five, was arrested and eventually convicted for her murder. A year after Murphy's death, the director of the National Women's Council of Ireland, Orla O'Connor, called the murder a 'watershed moment', and said that 'women really felt this was a point of no return.' She said, 'Male violence is a huge reality, and I think one of the things that really happened in the aftermath of Ashling Murphy's murder was all of the experiences that women spoke about, from sexual harassment to sexual violence, was part of everyday life and that's still the case.' She continued, 'There is so much more that we need to do, because we have the right to live in a society that's free from male violence. We all have to play our part in it, but we have a long road to go.'

p. 6, *I knew how powerful*: One American study in 2010 showed that 'personal, sensitizing' incidents are often key motivating factors for men who get involved with organizations or events dedicated to ending sexual or domestic violence. See Erin Casey and Tyler Smith, '"How Can I Not?": Men's Pathways to Involvement in Anti-Violence Against Women Work', *Violence Against Women*, 16(8), 2010, https://doi.org/10.1177/1077801210376749.

p. 9, *And the ones that do*: Men and boys who are the victims of sexual assault and rape are most often – but not always – victimized by other men. Over the past twenty years, brave testimonies from male survivors as well as a growing number of studies have demonstrated the prevalence of this problem and have helped to increase public awareness and decrease the stigma surrounding it. Services and treatment for male victims and survivors need much more support and funding. One specific area of male-on-male rape that does not receive much public attention is prison rape. In 2023 the *Guardian* reported, based on police data, that more than 1,000 rapes had occurred in prisons in England and Wales since 2010, a number that could be a serious undercount due to obstacles to reporting. See https://theguardian.com/society/2023/may/13/revealed-almost-1000-rapes-in-prisons-in-england-and-wales-since-2010. For more information about issues related to prison rape, go to the website of Just Detention International: https://justdetention.org/.

p. 11, *With initial funding*: For more information about the history of the MVP programme and the MVP model of bystander training, see my articles: 'Reconstructing Masculinity in the Locker Room: The Mentors in Violence Prevention Project', *Harvard Educational Review*, 65(2), 1995, pp. 163–75, https://doi.org/10.17763/haer.65.2.55533188520136u1; 'Bystander Training as Leadership Training: Notes on the Origins, Philosophy, and Pedagogy of the Mentors in Violence Prevention Model', *Violence Against Women*, 24(15), 2018, https://doi.org/10.1177/1077801217753322.

p. 19, *'There is a real consensus . . .'*: 'Majority of Men Support Gender Equality', Ipsos, 7 March 2019, https://ipsos.com/en-au/majority-men-support-gender-equality-ipsos-global-study.

p. 19, *'any harmful threat or act . . .'*: Office of Global Women's Issues, *United States Strategy to Prevent and Respond to Gender-Based Violence Globally 2022*, https://www.state.gov/reports/united-states-strategy-to-prevent-and-respond-to-gender-based-violence-globally-2022/.

p. 20, *When you insert the word 'men'*: The process of engaging men in primary prevention efforts remains challenging and complex. For one thing, a popular public health model championed by academic, governmental and community organizations has recast the specific issue of '(men's) violence against women' into the more generalized category of 'gender-based violence'. While this newer paradigm opens up space for making connections between women's experiences and those of LGBTQ people, as well as for the inclusion of boys and men as victims/survivors (as well as perpetrators), it risks decentring women, who remain the majority of victims/survivors worldwide.

p. 21, *According to Rape Crisis England and Wales*: See https://rapecrisis.org.uk/get-informed/statistics-sexual-violence; https://breathless-campaign.com.

p. 21, *During the COVID-19 pandemic*: Charlotte Proudman and Ffion Lloyd, 'The impact of COVID-19 on women and children in the UK who were victims of domestic abuse: a practitioner perspective', 23 November 2022, https://www.emerald.com/insight/content/doi/10.1108/JACPR-07-2022-0734/full/html.

p. 21, *In the US, domestic abuse hotlines*: National Coalition Against Domestic Violence, 'Domestic Violence', 2020, https://assets.speakcdn.com/assets/2497/domestic_violence-2020080709350855.pdf?1596828650457.

p. 23, *In his classic book*: Allan Johnson, *The Gender Knot: Unraveling our Patriarchal Legacy*, Temple University Press, 1997, 2014, p. 214.

p. 25, *To describe violence against women*: This line of reasoning applies to other areas of social justice – and often sparks contentious debates. For example, is it fair to assign the task of ending racism or undoing the deleterious effects of colonialism to its victims? Do Great Britain and other wealthy European colonial powers just get to walk away and bear no responsibility for centuries of human exploitation and wealth extraction from the Global South? What message does that send to white people or Europeans about what's expected of them? As Kiwi movie director Taika Waititi said to white people with reference to workplace diversity issues: 'Stop asking us [indigenous people] what to do, how to fix things, alright? . . . You fucking broke it, you fix it!'

p. 26, *Stewart said that he hadn't really faced*: Anna Moore, '"It's a Man's Problem": Patrick Stewart and the Men Fighting to End Domestic Violence', *Guardian*, 4 December 2018, https:// theguardian.com/ society/2018/dec/04/domestic-violence-abuse-patrick-stewart-david-challen-hart-brothers.

p. 29, *why should they bear . . . responsibility*: According to Harish Sadani, co-founder of the Mumbai-based Men Against Violence and Abuse (MAVA), and a leading anti-sexist male leader in India, 'Most people and institutions in India that work on gender-based violence – the Central and state governments, civil society bodies, international funding agencies, journalists – see men as "part of the problem". Indeed, India's patriarchal attitude that bestows countless privileges to men and sanctions restrictions on women is at the core of the problem. By and large men's violence against women is permissible.

'If men are part of the problem, how can we solve the problem unless men are also a part of the solution? What is desperately needed is to encourage men to actively stand against violence against women, while also interrogating how rigid gender roles negatively impact their own lives. Men are not born violent; they are conditioned by society's image of masculinity. It is high time men question the image and break out of it. We cannot expect women to become empowered without also sensitizing and transforming how men behave. They have to work hand in hand.'

From 'How Men Can Help Stop Violence Against Women', *The Wire*, 15 March 2020, https://thewire.in/gender/how-men-can-help-stop-violence-against-women.

p. 29, *According to feminist author Laura Bates*: Another famous feminist, Gloria Steinem, wrote in 1992 that women welcomed men's activism on these and other matters: 'Make no mistake about it, women want a men's movement. We are literally dying for it. If you doubt that, just listen to women's desperate testimonies of hope that the men in our lives will become more nurturing towards children, more able to talk about emotions, less hooked on a spectrum of control that extends from not listening through to violence.' (From the Foreword to *Women Respond to the Men's Movement*, edited by Kay Leigh Hagan.)

p. 29, *'hard work has been foisted . . .'*: Laura Bates, *Men Who Hate Women*, Simon & Schuster, 2020, p. 341.

p. 30, *Why not use gender-neutral terminology:* As I stated in the Author's Note at the beginning of this book, my intent is to centre men's violence against women and propose solutions to that enormous and persistent global problem. I am fully aware that men and non-binary people are also victims and survivors of gender-based violence, as are LGBTQ people. And of course people of all genders are capable of doing harm to others. I am also fully aware that despite mountains of evidence that demonstrates the connection between gender-based violence and systemic gender inequality, some people continue to insist that interpersonal violence is not really a 'gender' issue at all. I hope this book makes a convincing case that it is. In any event, I want to be clear that I believe victims/survivors of all genders deserve equal respect, justice, and access to the services and support they need.

p. 32, *has been around since at least the late 1970s*: Men's leadership in the struggle to end men's violence against women goes back much further. For example, the great nineteenth-century British philosopher John Stuart Mill, whose work I was introduced to as a young philosophy student, published a revolutionary manifesto against sexism and marital rape, *The Subjection of Women*, in 1869! Mill's essay – written with substantial input from his wife Harriet Taylor Mill – was an eloquent and deliberative plea for gender equality in an era when marital rape was legal and widespread. He wrote: 'When we consider how vast is the number of men, in any great country, who are little higher than brutes, and that this never prevents them from being able, through the law of marriage, to obtain a victim, the breadth and depth of human misery caused in this shape alone by the abuse of the institution swells to something appalling.'

p. 32, '*Act Like a Man Box*': The 'Man Box' exercise was developed by Paul Kivel and his Oakland Men's Project colleagues in the early 1980s, and adopted later as a signature concept by the US-based group A Call to Men. The exercise itself, which MVP trainers have used since the early 1990s, features a box drawn on a whiteboard. The facilitator asks men (and others) to describe the qualities of a 'real man', (e.g. *strong, stoic, provider, responsible*), which the facilitator writes inside the box. Then the facilitator asks for words to describe a man who does not demonstrate the characteristics inside the box (e.g. *soft, weak, sensitive*, and explicitly 'feminine' words such as *pussy, girlie*) and writes them outside the box. The inside-vs-outside-the-box structure sparks rich discussions about the ways in which men, young men, and boys are pressured to conform to certain dictates about 'manhood', and punished if they don't measure up.

p. 33, *challenging deeply rooted belief*: In 1976 – nearly a half-century ago – social psychologist Robert Brannon outlined what he called the four basic rules of masculinity. While it did not explicitly include men's behaviour towards women, this list has been highly influential in anti-sexist men's work. (Note: the brief commentary after each item was written by the sociologist Michael Kimmel and appeared in his 2008 book *Guyland*, pp. 45–46)

1) 'No sissy stuff'. Being a man means not being a sissy, not being perceived as weak, effeminate or gay. Masculinity is the relentless repudiation of the feminine.

2) 'Be a big wheel'. This rule refers to the centrality of success and power in the definition of masculinity. Masculinity is measured more by wealth, power and status than by any particular body part.

3) 'Be a sturdy oak'. What makes a man is that he is reliable in a crisis, and what makes him so reliable in a crisis is not that he is able to respond fully and appropriately to the situation at hand, but rather that he resembles an inanimate object. A rock, a pillar, a species of tree.

4) 'Give 'em hell'. Exude an aura of daring and aggression. Live life out on the edge. Take risks. Go for it. Pay no attention to what others think.

p. 36, *'The status quo is organized . . .'*: Allan Johnson, *The Gender Knot: Unraveling Our Patriarchal Legacy*, Temple University Press, 1997, 2014, p. 215.

p. 38, *a common law doctrine*: Alas, entrenched belief systems often retain influence long after shifts in legal theory and practice. Consider that although Matthew Hale wrote those words over 300 years ago, a 2018 YouGov survey found that more than a third of Britons over the age of 65 did not consider forced marital sex rape, along with 16 per cent of people aged 16–24. See https://yougov.co.uk/society/articles/22262-publics-attitudes-sexual-consent.

p. 43, *The connection between men's violence*: In his writing and speaking, author and White Ribbon Campaign co-founder Michael Kaufman has often elaborated on the many overlaps in patriarchal cultures between men's power and their pain: 'There's a paradox at the heart of men's lives. Men have power in male-dominated societies, but the ways we define and construct that power is the source of not only privilege but enormous negative consequences for men. Paradoxically, both this power and men's vulnerabilities are simultaneously sources of men's violence.' See https://soroptimistinternational. org/interview-michael-kaufman/.

p. 43, *They're all deeply interconnected*: Many men who use violence have themselves been victims of it – inside and outside their families in childhood and adolescence, growing up in conflict zones, serving in militaries, spending time in prison, etc. The traumatic injuries they've suffered don't excuse any abuse or violence they've inflicted on others, but understanding the ways in which traumatic experiences interact with masculine norms is a critical step forward in the search for solutions to the problem of men's violence. Along these lines, it is notable that Bessel Van der Kolk – one of the key figures in the trauma-informed care revolution and author of the mega bestseller *The Body Keeps the Score: Brain, Mind, and Body in the Healing of Trauma* – developed some of his early insights about trauma while working with (male) Vietnam veterans in Boston.

p. 45, *One such woman is Esta Soler*: 'The Interview: The Courage of Esta Soler', *Nob Hill Gazette*, 1 June 2021, https://nobhillgazette. com/people/the_interview/the-interview-the-courage-of-esta-soler/article_472b8451-2067-586f-ba73-422b6b6148bd.html.

p. 46, *a widely shared article in 2020*: Jessica Bennett, 'What if Instead of Calling People Out, We Called Them In?' *New York Times*, 19 November 2020, https://nytimes.com/2020/11/19/style/loretta-ross-smith-college-cancel-culture.html.

p. 49, *the UK's Domestic Abuse Act of 2021*: Crown Prosecution Service, 'Children Classed as Domestic Abuse Victims Under New Guidance', 5 December 2022, https://cps.gov.uk/cps/news/children-classed-domestic-abuse-victims-under-new-guidance.

p. 49, *Boys and men as sexual abuse survivors*: The report by the Centre of Expertise on Child Sexual Abuse entitled *The Scale and Nature of Child Sexual Abuse: Review of Evidence* is available here: https://csacentre.org.uk/app/uploads/2023/09/Scale-and-nature-review-of-evidence-2021.pdf.

p. 51, *In gender violence prevention work*: In recent decades, leaders in younger generations – Generations X, Y and Z – have expanded their efforts to pay special attention to the complex needs of women of colour and migrants. There is no one-size-fits-all solution for prevention, and this is equally true for survivors. Interventions have to be tailored to diverse communities and unique subcultures.

p. 51, *acknowledge ethnic/racial nuances and complexities*: This is the flip side of the argument that women of colour in the GBV field have been making for decades about women's lives and experiences. Andrea Simon, Executive Director of the Ending Violence Against Women Coalition, says working effectively with victims and survivors requires intersectional understanding and approaches. On the *Now and Men* podcast in April 2023, she put it this way: 'If you say you're going to stand up for women's rights and equality, you need to mean all women, and intersectionality needs to be practised, and it needs to be part of the way you think about the problem and what the solutions are . . . Different women have different health-seeking journeys, and that's impacted by race, by disability, sexuality. All the different things that make up our complex and wonderful lives will inform our own experiences of violence and abuse, and will affect our ability to access justice, and to access the support and services we need. [An intersectional approach] helps us to understand the really important work that specialist women's organizations – that are run by and for Black and minoritized women and migrant women and other marginalized communities – are so important to fund [. . .] because they are supporting women who are on some of the harshest ends of being impacted by violence, misogyny, sexism, racism and disablism.'

p. 52, *The great Nigerian feminist author*: Chimamanda Ngozi Adichie, *We Should All Be Feminists*, Anchor Books, 2014, p. 45.

p. 55, *In my experience, the first thing they need to hear*: For concrete examples, see 'Calling in All Men: 26 Recommendations for Engaging and Mobilizing Men to Prevent Violence and Advance Equity', by Lana M. Wells, available at: https://www.academia.edu/96001882/Calling_in_All_Men_26_Recommendations_for_Engaging_and_Mobilizing_Men_to_Prevent_Violence_and_Advance_Equity.

Chapter 2: Blaming Victims, Chasing Monsters

p. 56, *'The most rage-provoking element . . .'*: This Taylor Swift quote is drawn from an interview she did about the Long Pond Studio Sessions. It is available on YouTube at: https://www.youtube.com/watch?v=JM34N1ceyko. Gaslighting has traditionally been understood in psychological terms, but sociologist Paige Sweet argues that it is primarily a sociological phenomenon: 'Abusers mobilize gendered stereotypes; structural vulnerabilities related to race, nationality, and sexuality; and institutional inequalities against victims to erode their realities. These tactics are gendered in that they rely on the association of femininity with irrationality. Gaslighting offers an opportunity for sociologists to theorize under-recognized, gendered forms of power and their mobilization in interpersonal relationships.' See Paige Sweet, 'The Sociology of Gaslighting',

American Sociological Review, 84(5), 2019, pp. 851–75, https://doi. org/10.1177/0003122419874843.

p. 56, '. . .*nothing is more difficult than to understand him*': One of the most important and insightful books about men's violence is James Gilligan's *Violence: Reflections on a National Epidemic*, Putnam, 1996, Gilligan was a psychiatrist who worked for decades in the American prison system and was a long-time member of the Harvard Medical School faculty. In this book and others he describes the relationship between men's experience of shame and their commission of violence. He writes: 'I am convinced that violent behavior, even at its most apparently senseless, incomprehensible, and psychotic, is an understandable response to an identifiable, specifiable set of conditions; and that even when it seems motivated by "rational" self-interest, it is the end product of a series of irrational, self-destructive, and unconscious motives that can be studied, identified, and understood' (p. 102).

p. 58, *Signs at rallies*: Many Indian feminists were outraged at the victim-blaming that emerged in the trial of the men accused of the infamous Delhi gang rape in 2012. A lawyer for three of the defendants said that twenty-three-year-old Jyoti Singh and her male companion were 'wholly responsible' for the attack because they were an unmarried couple on the streets at night, the *Sydney Morning Herald* reported. 'Until today I have not seen a single incident or example of rape with a respected lady,' Manohar Lal Sharma told the newspaper.

p. 67, *it's always important to keep in mind*: It's worth noting that most men who abuse women are never held criminally responsible for their behaviour. A major Australian report on gender violence perpetration in 2022 said that 'the vast majority of domestic, family, and sexual violence is committed by individuals who are not – and probably never will be – identified or sanctioned by the authorities.' See https://research.qut.edu.au/centre-for-justice/wp-content/

uploads/sites/304/2023/01/Who-uses-domestic-family-and-sex-
ual-violence-how-and-why-The-State-of-Knowledge-Report-on-
Violence-Perpetration-2023.pdf.

p. 69, *it can be disturbing to realize*: BAFTA award-winning documentary filmmaker Deeyah Khan takes on the violent-man-as-
unknowable-monster caricature in a number of powerful films that
have aired on ITV. These include: *Jihad: A Story of the Others*, about
British jihadis; *White Right: Meeting the Enemy*, about American white
nationalists; and *Behind the Rage: America's Domestic Violence*, about
men convicted of killing their wives or domestic partners.

p. 70, *It's much easier to think about rapists*: Misogyny is deeply rooted
and gender-based violence is widespread, which means that many
'normal' guys have caused women harm, and a significant minority
have committed criminal acts. But a very small percentage of men
who physically or sexually abuse women are ever charged with a
crime, much less convicted and criminally punished. This raises
important questions about accountability and the possibilities for
redemption: what do these things look like? And who decides?
Racial justice and prison reform advocates have long argued for
non-carceral options for accountability. Are there ways to hold
abusers accountable that can be more effective than locking them
up? One approach that is growing in popularity in both the UK and
the States is restorative justice, where victims/survivors participate
in a mediated dialogue with their abusers. Throughout the process,
they get to decide not only what they need, but also what accountability – and possible redemption – looks like for the person who
hurt them.

p. 73, '*Rape culture is perpetuated . . .*': Charlamagne Tha God on *The Breakfast Club*. Available at: https://youtube.com/watch?v=7GeeC2ibD6g.

p. 73, '*[Boys] are bombarded . . .*': This quote is part of an essay by Jameela Jamil called 'Tell Him', available at https://iweigh community.com/tell-him-an-essay-by-jameela-jamil/.

p. 78, *Misogynous lyrics in rock and rap songs*: Byron Hurt's 2006 PBS documentary *Hip Hop: Beyond Beats and Rhymes* remains one of the touchstone critiques of hypermasculinity, misogyny and homophobia in rap music and culture. Hurt is a self-described hip-hop head from New York. He is also a former collegiate football quarterback and an original member of the MVP team.

p. 78, *Likewise, the topic of misogyny*: For a thoughtful discussion of the ways in which sexist jokes and comedy can make misogyny more socially acceptable, see R. Mallett et al., 'What Did He Mean by That?: Humor Decreases Attributions of Sexism and Confrontation of Sexist Jokes', *Sex Roles*, 75(5), 2016, pp. 272–84, https://doi.org/10.1007/s11199-016-0605-2.

p. 81, *Feminist theorists and media literacy educators*: Dr Jean Kilbourne's original illustrated slide lecture and subsequent educational video *Killing Us Softly: Advertising's Image of Women* (1979) is a foundational work in the field of modern media literacy education. My first slide lecture and film, *Tough Guise* (1999), drew inspiration from Kilbourne's work.

p. 82, *more than a third of UK women*: Alys Harte, '"A man tried to choke me during sex without warning"', BBC News, 27 November 2019, https://bbc.com/news/uk-50546184.

p. 83, *University of Sydney senior lecturer Samuel Shpall*: Walter Marsh, '"The real thing almost didn't turn me on enough": How is online porn shaping the sex lives of young men?', *Guardian*, 27 January 2024, https://theguardian.com/society/2024/jan/28/australia-e-safety-commissioner-online-porn-study-data?.

p. 84, *One 2010 study showed that 88 per cent*: Ana Bridges et al., 'Aggression and Sexual Behavior in Best-Selling Pornography Videos: A Content Analysis Update', *Violence Against Women*, 16(10), 2010, pp. 1065–85, https://doi.org/10.1177/1077801210382866.

p. 84, *average age at which kids were exposed to porn*: 'Teens and Pornography', Common Sense Media, https:// commonsensemedia.org/ sites/default/files/research/report/2022-infographic-teens-and-pornography-research-eng-web_1.pdf.

p. 84, *'this is predominantly a gender-based crime . . .'*: Vikram Dodd, 'Children Now "Biggest Perpetrators of Sexual Abuse Against Children"', *Guardian*, 10 January 2024, https://www.theguardian.com/society/2024/jan/10/children-now-biggest-perpetrators-of-sexual-abuse-against-children.

p. 85, *'Exposure to porn increases . . .'*: Michael Flood, 'Young Men Using Pornography', in Karen Boyle (ed.), *Everyday Pornography*, Routledge, 2010, https://researchgate.net/profile/Michael-Flood-4/publication/234028315_Young_Men_Using_Porn/links/0fcfd50e6395cafaaf000000/Young-Men-Using-Porn.pdf.

p. 86, *Gail Dines says in her public lectures*: From personal communication with author.

p. 86, *Laura Bates says that when she visits schools*: Bates, *Men Who Hate Women*, p. 271.

p. 86, *An analysis of porn titles*: Fiona Vera-Gray et al., 'Sexual Violence as a Sexual Script in Mainstream Online Pornography', *British Journal of Criminology*, 61(5), 2021, pp. 1243–60, https://doi.org/10.1093/bjc/azab035.

p. 87, *'live in a culture that sees female pain . . .'*: Lili Loofbourow, 'The Female Price of Male Pleasure', *The Week*, 25 January 2018, https://theweek.com/articles/749978/female-price-male-pleasure.

p. 87, *Peggy Orenstein describes a conversation*: Peggy Orenstein, *Boys & Sex: Young Men on Hookups, Love, Porn, Consent, and Navigating the New Masculinity*, Harper, 2020, p. 28.

p. 87, *porn often functions as a how-to guide*: In her book *Pornland*, Gail Dines writes: 'If we refuse to accept the easy answer that men have a natural predisposition to get off on hurting women, then we have to look to the culture for answers as to why some men seek out and enjoy gonzo. We have to ask, What is it about male socialization and masculinity that helps prepare them – or, I would say, groom them – into seeking out and masturbating to such images? The answers do not lie within individual men; rather, they are found in the culture that we all live in. Porn is not something that stands outside of us: it is deeply embedded in our structures, identities, and relationships. This did not happen overnight, and there is a story to tell about how we got to the point that mainstream Internet porn has become so hateful and cruel' (p. xxix).

p. 87, *Perhaps the most alarming aspect*: Pressure on the neck can be a recipe for disaster. According to the *Journal of Emergency Medicine*, strangulation can result in such injuries as memory loss, vision problems, nose bleeds, miscarriage and suicidal thoughts (https://doi.org/10.1016/S0736-4679(01)00398-5). Moreover, the Training Institute on Strangulation Prevention calls strangulation 'an ultimate form of power and control where the batterer can demonstrate control over the victim's next breath'. This is what is being normalized under the euphemism 'choking'. On TikTok, which attracts a quarter of a billion teens and tweens monthly, millions of viewers have watched adolescent girls dancing to music with the tag #ChokeMe. Violent sex has become so mainstream that young people who resist 'choking' are regularly shamed as uptight 'vanilla' prudes. (The incidence of choking/strangulation is also high in LGBTQ relationships.) For more information about the normalization of non-consensual strangulation, go to the Breathless Campaign website: https://breathlesscampaign.com.

p. 88, *significant negative health effects*: For more information and analysis of the normalization of sexual strangulation, see Orenstein's article 'The Troubling Trend in Teenage Sex', *New York Times*, 12 April 2024, https://nytimes.com/2024/04/12/opinion/choking-teen-sex-brain-damage.html.

p. 88, *a major homicide risk factor*: N. Glass et al., 'Non-Fatal Strangulation is an Important Risk Factor for Homicide of Women', *Journal of Emergency Medicine*, 35(3), 2008, pp. 329–35, https://doi.org/10.1016/j.jemermed.2007.02.065.

p. 88, *many young women didn't realize*: Fiona Vera-Gray on the *Now and Men* podcast, 8 October 2021, https://now-and-men.captivate.fm/episode/mens-violence-against-women.

p. 90, *'Over the years I have come to understand . . .'*: Gail Dines, *Pornland: How Porn Has Hijacked Our Sexuality*, Beacon Press, 2010, p. 80.

p. 91, *Many men are deeply conflicted*: In her 2015 TEDx Talk, 'Growing Up in a Pornified Culture,' Gail Dines describes the process of sexually curious young boys going to a porn website. She quotes from the promotional copy of a well-known site called Gag Me Then Fuck Me: 'We take gorgeous young bitches and do what every man would really like to do – we make them gag.' 'Now, think about this', says Dines. '[The boy who goes to this site] is twelve years old, he is going into manhood, he is aroused, this is telling him, "You wanna be a male? This is your entrée into masculinity. This is the price you pay to be masculine." In that boy's stomach is a toxic stew because he's aroused, but he is also ashamed, and he is also scared, and he is also angry, and he feels enormous shame that he is aroused, and nobody has said to him, "This is not who you are." Because the pornographers say to him: "This is who you are. This is what you want.

Because we take gorgeous young bitches, and we do what every man would really like to do." But you know what? That's not true. I know that's not true, and I know that is not true because feminists are men's best friends, because we believe more in men than the pornographers do. And you know how I know that the pornographers don't tell the truth about men? I know that as a feminist, I know that as a scholar, and above all, I know that as a mother of a son. My son is worth better than this. If my son is, then I believe your son is too.' The talk is available on YouTube at https://youtube.com/watch?v=_YpHNImNsx8.

p. 91, *'Much of the guilt and shame . . .'*: Robert Jensen, 'Lost in a Sea of Pixels: Men, Pornography, and the Illusion of Control', *Public Square Magazine*, 15 May 2023, https://robertwjensen.org/articles/lost-in-a-sea-of-pixels-men-pornography-and-the-illusion-of-control/.

p. 92, *The misogynous manosphere*: For an analysis of the manosphere, see Equimundo, *The Manosphere, Rewired: Understanding Masculinities Online and Pathways for Healthy Connection*, 2024, https://equimundo.org/resources/manosphere-rewired/.

p. 94, *'I'm a realist . . .'*: Antoinette Radford, 'Who is Andrew Tate? The Self-Proclaimed Misogynist Influencer', BBC News, 12 March 2024, https://bbc.com/news/uk-64125045.

p. 94, *In a 2022 interview with Barstool Sports*: Available at https://youtube.com/watch?v=RmKpGasht9c.

p. 94, *Stories began to appear in national newspapers*: Stephanie Wescott et al., 'The Problem of Anti-Feminist "Manfluencer" Andrew Tate in Australian Schools: Women Teachers' Experiences of Resurgent Male Supremacy', *Gender and Education*, 36(2), 2024, pp. 167–82, https://doi.org/10.1080/09540253.2023.2292622.

p. 94, *By the end of the pandemic in 2022*: Maya Oppenheim, 'One in Four Young Men Agree with Andrew Tate's Views on Women, Poll Finds',

Independent, 22 May 2023, https://independent.co.uk/news/uk/home-news/andrew-tate-women-masculinity-romania-b2342084.html.

p. 95, *'not just an exogenous shock . . .'*: Alice Evans, 'What Prevents & What Drives Gendered Ideological Polarisation', 27 January 2024, https://ggd.world/p/what-prevents-and-what-drives-gendered.

p. 97, *one way to counteract the malign influence*: Among the numerous books on various aspects of men's health by pro-feminist men (and others) are Will Courtenay's *Dying to be Men*; Justin Baldoni's *Man Enough*; Yarneccia Dyson et al. (eds), *Black Men's Health*; Ronald Levant and Shana Pryor's *The Tough Standard*; Michael Kimmel and Michael Messner's *Men's Lives* series; and Rob Okun (ed.), *Voice Male*. Organizations whose work addresses men's health and men's violence include global organizations like Equimundo and Movember, India's Men Against Violence and Abuse, South Africa's Sonke Gender Justice, Sweden's MÄN and the US-based A Call to Men.

Chapter 4: Pushback

p. 101, *You're overlooking male victims!*: There is extensive literature on the violent victimization of men and boys. This includes instances when men are the victims of violence by women. The profeminist site XY Online, founded and curated by Dr Michael Flood, includes a detailed list of references to this literature. See https://xyonline.net/books/bibliography/27-violence-and-responses-violence/l-when-men-are-subject-violence

p. 105, *'We forgive Us . . .'*: Robert Sapolsky, *Behave: The Biology of Humans at Our Best and Worst*, Penguin, 2017, p. 395.

p. 105, *Moreover, sociological analysis*: 'Feminist sociological analyses of woman abuse that prioritize the concept of patriarchy, especially in North America, have leveled off or declined in the last twelve years. Most violence against women authors are now based in psychology, psychiatry, nursing, and medicine. This is not to say that these disciplines did not also advance the field. They have, but they now dominate it in North America and other parts of the world. What makes this highly problematic is that these ways of knowing focus more on individuals and lose sight of how broader social, cultural, political, and economic forces shape violence against women and societal reactions to its many shapes and forms.' Walter DeKeseredy, 'Bringing Feminist Sociological Analyses of Patriarchy Back to the Forefront of the Study of Woman Abuse', *Violence Against Women*, 27(5), 2021, pp. 621–38, https://doi.org/10.1177/10778012209558485.

p. 106, *This false equivalence fallacy*: For a rebuttal of the false equivalence fallacy in domestic abuse perpetration, see Michael S. Kimmel, '"Gender Symmetry" in Domestic Violence: A Substantive and Methodological Research Review"', *Violence Against Women*, 8(11), 2002, pp. 1332–63, https://doi.org/10.1177/107780102237407.

p. 106, *The writer and Remaking Manhood podcaster*: Mark Greene, 'Men: Our Silence Is Killing Us', 20 September 2023, https://linkedin.com/pulse/men-our-silence-killingus-mark-greene/.

p. 108, *'I . . . don't buy the argument . . .'*: On the *Conversations with Tyler* podcast, 13 February 2019, https://conversationswithtyler.com/episodes/jordan-peterson/.

p. 108, *He once suggested to an interviewer*: Vice interview, available at https://youtube.com/watch?v=S9dZSlUjVls.

p. 108, *He professed sympathy*: See https://youtube.com/watch?v=rGsZ_HI_q1M.

p. 110, *Many men would rather go along*: 'The men lashing out at women online, the ones who use misogyny and racism and abuse to fiercely protect what they see as their territory, consider themselves to be the good guys. But it's like they don't realize that racism, misogyny, homophobia, transphobia, ableism and all the other bigoted views they uphold and gleefully enforce are, you know, *what the baddies do*. They spent their youths daydreaming about being Jedi Masters, and they haven't yet realized that they've grown up to be Stormtroopers, mindlessly doing the bidding of whichever evil leader they're acting in service to. The funniest thing is that, in the real world, they would dismiss all their heroes as cucks and white knights.' Clementine Ford, *Boys Will Be Boys: Power, Patriarchy and Toxic Masculinity*, Oneworld Publications, 2019, p. 98.

p. 111, *The therapist and bestselling author*: Terry Real's first book, *I Don't Want to Talk About It: Overcoming the Secret Legacy of Male Depression* (1997), was a groundbreaking exploration of men's emotional and relational health. In several other books about relationships, he draws on his many years of experience as a couples therapist. His client list includes Bruce Springsteen and his wife Patti Scialfa. In the foreword to Real's book *Us* (2022), Springsteen writes that for him and Patti, Real has been a guide 'through the dark forest and down to that river of life'.

p. 111, *71 per cent of men surveyed*: Equimundo, *State of American Men 2023: From Crisis and Confidence to Hope*, 2023, https://equimundo.org/resources/state-of-american-men/.

Chapter 5: Language Matters

p. 120, *how to overhaul language usage*: See https://ipso.co.uk/resources/sexual-offences-guidance;https://nsvrc.org/sexual-violence-reporting-tools.

p. 120, *People who run court-mandated groups*: The men, women and others who work in programmes for men who use violence in their intimate relationships are some of the most important front-line workers in the struggle against domestic and sexual violence. Their voices are critical in conversations about solutions, because they know so much about what drives men to use violence; they're in dialogue with such men every day. Yet their voices are rarely heard on TV or in mainstream discourse about this subject or about the many overlaps and intersections between men's violence against women in relationships and a number of other social problems, e.g. gang violence, drug and alcohol abuse, homelessness.

p. 124, *'Violence against women and girls . . .'*: António Guterres, 'Secretary-General's Remarks on the International Day for the Elimination of Violence Against Women', 25 November 2020, https://un.org/sg/en/content/sg/statement/2020-11-25/secretary-generals-remarks-the-international-day-for-the-elimination-of-violence-against-women-delivered.

p. 125, *'It is unacceptable . . .'*: European Commission, 'Violence Against Women: The European Union Establishes an EU-Wide Helpline Number and Calls to End Violence Against Women Worldwide', 24 November 2022, https://ec.europa.eu/commission/presscorner/detail/en/statement_22_7113.

p. 125, *Pope Francis met with*: Lisa Zengarini, 'Pope: Violence Against Women Must Be Addressed Through a Joint Effort', *Vatican News*, 26 November 2022, https://vaticannews.va/en/pope/news/2022-11/pope-violence-against-women-to-be-addressed-with-joint-effort.html.

p. 130, *A case in point was an opinion piece*: Paul Zeise, 'Adults at Hockey Game Failed to Protect Goalie', *Pittsburgh Post-Gazette*, 3 November 2023, https://www.post-gazette.com/sports/paul-zeise/2021/11/03/Armstrong-Mars-hockey-game-goalie-chants/stories/202111020168.

p. 133, *I try to avoid using it*: Well before the mythopoetic era, a now largely forgotten predecessor to 'toxic masculinity' was the humorous term 'testosterone poisoning', which first appeared in a satirical essay by the American TV and film actor Alan Alda that was published in *Ms. Magazine* all the way back in 1975. In the essay, entitled 'What Every Woman Should Know About Men', Alda wrote that 'everyone knows that testosterone, the so-called male hormone, is found in both men and women. What is not so well known, is that men have an overdose . . . Until recently it has been thought that the level of testosterone in men is normal simply because they have it. But if you consider how abnormal their *behavior* is, then you are led to the hypothesis that almost all men are suffering from *testosterone poisoning.*' A key warning sign of testosterone poisoning, according to Alda, is how you answer the question 'Does violence play a big part in your life?' He continued: 'Before you answer, count up how many hours you watched football, ice hockey, and children's cartoons this year on television. When someone crosses you, do you wish you could stuff his face full of your fist? . . . if so, you're in big trouble, fella.'

p. 135 *'our boys are capable . . .'*: From Don McPherson, 'Aspirational Masculinity', https://donmcpherson.com/dgm-blog/aspirational-masculinity (retrieved 13 July 2024).

p. 136, *we need to 'celebrate the good parts'*: Ben Hurst, 'Boys Won't Be Boys: Boys Will Be What We Teach Them to Be', TEDx Talk, December 2018, https://ted.com/talks/ben_hurst_boys_won_t_be_boys_boys_will_be_what_we_teach_them_to_be.

Chapter 6: The Bystander Approach: How Everyone Can Make a Difference

p. 138, *have been developing bystander training*: Bystander training was a concrete educational response to the idea that men had a bigger role to play in the prevention of gender-based violence. It might be surprising to read, but engaging men in this work was an increasingly urgent topic of conversation more than thirty years ago in pockets of activist agitation in the US, Canada, the UK and elsewhere. For example, in 1990 a Boston-based anti-sexist men's group I led was part of a coalition that organized a week-long series of public events on the Boston Common and elsewhere, called 'Ceasefire Action Week: A Call for Men to Stop Violence Against Women', that included a packed workshop entitled 'Interrupting Sexism: Men Confronting Men'. The workshop's description read: 'Men confronting each other to stop sexism is still a rare event. Partly because we are afraid of ridicule and violence, even men who are against sexism often remain silent. This workshop invites men to share their experience with confrontation and to find successful methods.' Among other contemporaneous developments was the founding of the White Ribbon Campaign in Toronto in 1991, which became the world's largest public anti-sexist men's initiative, and the founding of Men Against Violence and Abuse (MAVA) in Mumbai in 1993, one of India's first anti-sexist men's groups. Both organizations are still going strong today.

p. 140, *Baroness Louise Casey's highly critical report*: Baroness Casey, *An Independent Review into the Standards of Behaviour and Internal Culture of the Metropolitan Police Service: Final Report*, March 2023, https://met.police.uk/SysSiteAssets/media/downloads/met/about-us/baroness-casey-review/update-march-2023/baroness-casey-review-march-2023a.pdf.

p. 141, *That led us to incorporate and adapt*: In the second year of the MVP programme, we expanded the model to include women as bystanders. What can they do to interrupt and challenge abusive behaviour, support targets and survivors, provide leadership to younger women, etc.? Today, MVP and its many spin-off programmes address the role of bystanders in instances of harassment, abuse and violence committed and experienced by people across the gender and sexual identity spectrum – including many situations in which men are the victims – without losing sight of the fact that men comprise the vast majority of abusers, and men's violence against women is the primary focus.

p. 146, *Graham Goulden, a former Chief Inspector*: Goulden played a central role in bringing MVP and bystander training to Scotland in the early 2010s by helping to convene a collaboration between the Violence Reduction Unit and the education ministry. The result has been the groundbreaking MVP Scotland initiative. More information on Goulden's work can be found at grahamgoulden.com. Information about MVP Scotland is available at: https://education.gov.scot/resources/mentors-for-violence-prevention-mvp-an-overview/.

p. 152, *a body of research*: Some of the early (1980s) research in social norms theory addressed the ways in which the drinking habits of university students were influenced by their perception of group norms for alcohol consumption. This research led to public health interventions beginning in the 1990s such as messaging campaigns that provided an accurate accounting of the actual and not merely perceived norms on campus. This model was later applied to campus-based sexual assault prevention, especially with men.

Chapter 7: What Leaders Can Do

p. 157, *'When a man speaks up . . .'*: From David G. Smith and W. Brad Johnson, *Good Guys*, Harvard Business Review Press, 2020, pp. 124–5.

p. 157, *'Ending this epidemic of violence . . .'*: Brianna Boecker, 'Anthony Albanese Calls for Men to "Take Responsibility" for Australia's Epidemic of Violence Against Women', Women's Agenda, 7 February 2024,https://womensagenda.com.au/politics/local/anthony-albanese-calls-for-men-to-take-responsibility-for-australias-epidemic-of-violence-against-women/.

p. 159, *'the head coach is ultimately responsible . . .'*: Dustin Jones, 'North-western Football Coach Pat Fitzgerald is Fired Following Hazing Investigation', NPR, 11 July 2023, https://npr.org/2023/07/11/1186971916/northwestern-university-football-hazing-pat-fitzgerald-fired.

p. 159, *whether ultimate authority*: While many in the US military opposed making changes to existing policy, public pressure on Congress and the White House had built over the past decade after many tragic sexual assault and domestic homicide incidents that advocates felt were poorly handled by military authorities. In what was seen as a major victory for survivors and a big step forward for institutional accountability, in 2023 President Joe Biden signed an executive order with bipartisan support that vested binding power in the independent prosecutors.

p. 160, *a culture of discrimination*: Maite Fernández Simon, 'Watchdog Report: London Police Officers Engaged in Misogynistic, Racist, Discriminatory Behavior', *Washington Post*, 2 February 2022, https://www.washingtonpost.com/world/2022/02/02/london-metro-police-misogyny-report/.

p. 165, *Unfortunately, women at the forefront*: Traditional leadership lit-erature rarely acknowledges – much less analyses – women's leadership in the domestic abuse and sexual assault movements. This is especially true for the contributions of women of colour. For a further discussion, see the article I co-wrote with Shelley Eriksen, 'Credit where it is due: gender violence prevention as a leadership issue', eds. Sherylle Tan and Lisa DeFrank-Cole, in *A Research Agenda for Gender and Leadership*, Edward Elgar Publishing, 2023.

p. 169, *'imagine a society . . .'*: Jessica Elgot, 'Keir Starmer Promises to Halve Violence Against Women as Part of Crime "Mission" ', *Guardian*, 23 March 2023, https://theguardian.com/politics/2023/

mar/23/keir-starmer-promises-to-halve-violence-against-women-as-part-of-labour-crime-mission.

p. 170, '*Whether in politics, in the office . . .*': Humza Yousaf, 'Misogynists Like Andrew Tate Hold Sway Over Thousands of Men and Boys. Male Leaders Like Me Must Address That', *Guardian*, 15 August 2023, https://theguardian.com/commentisfree/2023/aug/15/misogynists-andrew-tate-humza-yousaf-men-pain-male-leaders.

p. 171, *Where is the sense of urgency*: The late and enormously influential radical feminist writer Andrea Dworkin gave a famous speech in 1983 to a group of 500 men (and a few women) at a 'National Organization for Changing Men' conference in St Paul, Minnesota. In the talk, entitled 'I Want a Twenty-Four-Hour Truce During Which There is No Rape', she said, 'I speak for many feminists, not only myself, when I tell you that I am tired of what I know and sad beyond any words I have about what has already been done to women up to this point, now, up to 2:24pm on this day, here in this place. And I want one day of respite, one day off, one day in which no new bodies are piled up, one day in which no new agony is added to the old, and I am asking you to give it to me. And how could I ask you for less: it is so little. And how could you offer me less: it is so little. Even in wars, there are days of truce. Go and organize a truce. Stop your side for one day. I want a twenty-four-hour truce during which there is no rape. I dare you to try it. I demand that you try it. I don't mind begging you to try it. What else could you possibly be here to do? What else could this movement possibly mean? What else could matter so much?'

p. 176, '*Most men in leadership positions . . .*': Ray Arata, *Showing Up: How Men Can Become Effective Allies in the Workplace*, Diversion Books, 2022, p. 189.

p. 179, *The idea was to have early morning leadership gatherings*: Some of the earliest such breakfasts were held in Edmonton and Calgary, in the province of Alberta, Canada. They were organized by the Alberta

Council of Women's Shelters, with whom I have worked for nearly two decades. Several retired National Hockey League players and team owners participated.

p. 181, *Leadership isn't always formal*: Barbershops are an important social institution – especially in communities of colour – and barbers are often well-respected members of the community and trusted confidants of their clientele. As a result, a number of initiatives around the world have sought to train and support barbers to utilize their unique 'informal leadership' platform to address domestic abuse and other serious matters with their male clients. One of the more notable of these initiatives was in Christchurch, New Zealand, where a barber named Mataio Taimalelagi (Matt Brown), a man of Samoan descent and himself a survivor of family and childhood abuse, began by talking honestly and empathetically with his clients about those topics and more over a decade ago. He and his wife Sarah launched the 'She Is Not Your Rehab' campaign in 2019 and were awarded the New Zealand Order of Merit in 2022.

p. 184, *Exercise proactive leadership*: A 2018 report by the American National Academies of Sciences, Engineering, and Medicine included a series of recommendations for leaders. One was that 'college and university presidents, provosts, deans, department chairs, and program directors must make the reduction and prevention of sexual harassment an explicit goal of their tenure. They should publicly state that the reduction and prevention of sexual harassment will be among their highest priorities, and they should engage students, faculty, and staff (and, where appropriate, the local community) in their efforts' (p. 7). The report went on to say that 'compliance with legal requirements is not enough; aggressive, highly visible managerial implementation of anti-harassment policies and procedures in a concerted way not only raises awareness that policies and procedures are in place but also signals organizational commitment to reducing harassment. In other words, leaders' behavior instructs members of the community about what to expect around sexual harassment, and any formal policies will be interpreted through the organizational climate they create and maintain' (p. 148).

Chapter 8: Where Do We Go from Here?

p. 189, *Get Help*: Some individuals who are physically and/or sexually abusive come from families with a long history of abuse. The good news is that some of the most important social change work also takes place within families. It can be immensely stressful and isolating to confront painful truths about the intergenerational transmission of trauma. If you're in a position to do this, or to support a family member doing so, try to take the first step. Consult with a social worker, therapist, or another professional you trust about options available to you. Be bold. As the therapist and author Terry Real says, 'Family pathology is like a fire in the woods taking down all in front of it until someone turns to face the flames.'

p. 197, *'parties shall take the necessary . . .'*: https://edoc.coe.int/en/violence-against-women/7140-preventing-violence-against-women-article-12-of-the-istanbul-convention.html.

p. 199, *back in the 1980s, the men against sexism*: Julie Bindel, 'Want to be a True Feminist Ally? Learn from These Men', *Al Jazeera*, 20 January 2023, https://aljazeera.com/opinions/2023/1/20/want-to-be-a-true-feminist-ally-learn-from-these-men.

p. 200, *real sustainable change requires*: Equimundo, *State of American Men 2023*.

Index